WISDOM THAT
WORKS

WISDOM THAT
WORKS

How to Use the Messages of *Conversations with God*

ANNIE SIMS

Foreword by Neale Donald Walsch

RAINBOW RIDGE
BOOKS

Cover and interior design by Jonathan Friedman / Frame25 Productions
Cover photo © snapshopped c/o Shutterstock.com

Published by:
Rainbow Ridge Books, LLC
1056 Commodore Drive
Virginia Beach, VA 23454
www.rainbowridgebooks.com

If you are unable to order this book from your local
bookseller, you may order directly from the distributor.

Square One Publishers, Inc.
115 Herricks Road
Garden City Park, NY 11040
877-900-BOOK

Library of Congress Control Number: 2019937997

ISBN 978-1-937907-61-7

10 9 8 7 6 5 4 3 2 1

Printed in India through Nutech Print Services

CONTENTS

Foreword   ix

About This Book   xi

Introduction   xiii

How to Get the Most From This Book   xix

Chapter 1: The Basics   1

Lesson #1: Oneness   1

Lesson #2: Abundance   9

Lesson #3: Nothing You Have To Do   16

Lesson #4: Divine Communication   20

Chapter 2: Creation & Purpose   35

Lesson #1: Creating Your Own Reality   35

Lesson #2: The Three Tools of Creation   48

Lesson #3: The Be-Do-Have Paradigm   59

Lesson #4: The Purpose of Life   71

Chapter 3: Dispelling a Few Misconceptions   81

Lesson #1: Right and Wrong   81

Lesson #2: God's Wants & Requirements   90

Lesson #3: Damnation   101

Lesson #4: Death   111

Chapter 4: Larger Understandings   131

Lesson #1: Time and Space   131

Lesson #2: Victims and Villains   141

Lesson #3: The Law of Opposites   148

Lesson #4: Absolute Truth   160

Chapter 5: The Power of Threes   169

Lesson #1: The 3 Core Concepts of Holistic Living   169

Lesson #2: The 3 Levels of Awareness   185

Lesson #3: The 3 Basic Principles of Life   193

Lesson #4: The 3 Declarations of Empowerment   201

Chapter 6: Who You Are & Moving Beyond the Illusions   213

Lesson #1: The Totality of You   213

Lesson #2: The Ten Illusions of Humans   223

Lesson #3: The Five Fallacies About God and Life   232

Lesson #4: The Five Steps To Peace   243

Afterword   251

Recommended Resources   253

Praise for Wisdom that Works: The CWG Online School   259

Acknowledgements   261

About the Author   263

For Neale, who helped me remember what I knew before
I got here, and for Greg, who helps me remember to use it.

FOREWORD

For years, every time I would pick up one of the *Conversations with God* books and dip into the dialogue, I would think to myself, "I wish there was a way to *step through* this material, one spiritual principle at a time. There should be a way to *functionalize* the messages that have been given to us here."

Then into my life along came a lady named Annie Sims. She's told here of how we first met and what happened after she and her husband Greg and I became friends. But what she hasn't told you (because she couldn't possibly know the depth of it) is what it has meant to me to have her do what she wound up doing.

Annie Sims wound up opening the way for people to turn what's found on the pages of CWG from Concept into Experience, making it a real part of everyday life and not just a collection of wonderful ideas. This has meant more to me than you could know, because now *I* know that *Conversations with God* will no longer remain simply thousands of words between book covers, but can now be transformed into thousands of moments bringing thousands of joys into thousands of lives.

Suddenly there is a road map for one of the greatest journeys that anyone could ever take—the journey of creation and self-realization. Here is a traveler's guide to all the points of interest along the path; a set of directions on which way one can turn at life's intersections.

Through the years Annie's in-depth and ongoing study of the 3,000+ pages of the CWG dialogues has made her a wonderfully clear teacher and an inspired spiritual mentor, with a magical ability to form esoteric commentaries into practical recommendations and powerful suggestions that every person can begin to use immediately.

I am grateful to my friend of the soul for creating the online course from which this text emerged, and the book itself, refining the information and offering personal observations that make it come alive through her gift of adding a sweet, gentle and often humorous human touch to divine insights, producing, truly, wisdom that works.

Enjoy what you are about to read. It will serve you now, and through all the remaining years of your life.

—Neale Donald Walsch

ABOUT THIS BOOK

Wisdom that Works is a derivative work, based on Neale Donald Walsch's best-selling *Conversations with God* series of books. In them, Neale asserts that when he asked questions of Deity, he received answers in his mind.

He wrote down the question and answer sessions for several years before a publisher pounced on them, knowing that the information contained great wisdom for the world.

It is not a prerequisite that you read any or all of the *Conversations with God* books before reading this one. It is also not necessary that you believe Neale "heard" God speaking to him. Heck, you don't even have to believe in God in the first place. I know. I was on the fence about it, for a long time, until *Conversations With God, Book 3* was literally pushed into my hands.

But God believes in you, whether you know it or not. And I think you'll find plenty of ideas here you can use to create a happier experience of life, regardless.

Lastly, a number of the concepts you'll find in this book may, at first glance, give you pause—to say the least—as they are quite spiritually advanced. Some may even seem controversial, but doesn't growth begin by exploring daring new ideas? I kindly ask you, the reader, to try to keep an open mind and heart as you, hopefully, sally forth through this book all the way to the end.

INTRODUCTION

What you hold in your hand began with a telephone call from my friend and spiritual mentor, Neale Donald Walsch, inviting me to create a course for what would become Wisdom that Works: The CWG Online School. He asked me to take the Core Concepts from his best-selling *Conversations with God* books and write lessons and assignments for each. The program would be self-contained on its own website where students would post their work, and I would serve as their instructor and give them feedback—all of this would be done online inside the program. I absolutely loved writing those lessons and was thrilled that the ideas came easily. I have the thought that if something I'm doing flows freely and joyfully, I am on track, aligned with my soul's highest expression. I titled the course "Wisdom that Works," because what good is spiritual knowledge if you don't know how to use it to create a better life? As Neale told me that day, "Experience is the bridge between knowledge and wisdom." He also told me, "This will someday become a book." As I hung up the phone and pondered his words, I knew I had just received information that was both profound and prophetic, from the most spiritually clear person I've ever known.

What preceded that request was one of the two greatest gifts in my life, and it, too, came at the beckoning of Neale Donald Walsch. In December 2008 my husband Greg and I attended the Conversations with God Foundation's year-end retreat. On the last afternoon, Neale announced to the room, "When we come back from the break, I'm going to show you how I have a conversation with God." He said, "If you could ask God only one question, what would it be?" I immediately knew what I wanted to ask, as it had been a subject of great confusion and distress that I'd carried my entire adult life. When we returned to the room, the lights were dim, and angelic music was playing softly in the background. Neale had us each write out our question on a notepad, then put it under our chairs. He proceeded to guide us in a meditation so deep, we were able to quiet our minds from their incessant chatter. Once we were all in a very still, receptive state, he quietly said, "Now, take out your pen and paper and write down the first thing that comes to you." As I wrote what I heard in my mind, the tears flowed and flowed. The cathartic answer I received rang so utterly true to my heart and soul, I knew I need never live "in the dark" again:

Q: How can I be fully happy in spite of animals' suffering?

> *Just BE happy. Trust the process. Go on faith.*
>
> *They come home to me, too. They come here (to Earth) because they choose to. They are not unhappy, you just think they are. They are loved and they know it at a soul level. Don't worry about them. I take care of them just as I take care of you—all of you. They are joyous in coming here just as you were.*

*And you thought Neale had all the answers. I talk to you, too. I always have, and
you know it. That's me you hear at night when you get quiet.*

When Greg and others at the retreat shared what they had "heard," I was amazed at the beautifully articulate way God also "spoke" to them. I realized for the first time that it isn't only Neale who can hear what I now affectionately call *The Voice*. That wonderfully clear, guiding wisdom is available to all of us, all the time.

Greg and I loved the process so much we kept doing it after we got home, especially when life presented us with challenges. We would write out any questions we had, thanking God in advance for any answers that might come through, then close our eyes, get very still and listen. As Psalms wisely says, "Be still and know." We would then write out any thoughts that came to us, one phrase at a time, and they often flowed as question and answer sessions. We would never stop to read what we'd written until we felt complete. We always gained clarity and peace of mind following these conversations with God (we call them our "CWGs"), and over time, we learned to trust and act on whatever guidance we received.

The Voice—that still, small voice that comes through in our CWGs—is quite different from our normal way of speaking. It usually comes through in the second person point of view, as if someone is talking *to* us. The language is often more eloquent than our own, and the messages always more wise. They often contain new ideas we have never before considered that serve to greatly improve and enhance our experience of life.

Eventually, as I began working more with Neale and his team, I started offering my own version of his "How to Have Your Own Conversation with God" process in workshops at Unity Churches and Centers For Spiritual Living. I'm such a firm believer in its power to change our lives for the better, I also recommend it to students in my online school and to life coaching clients. As I've worked with people in many different countries, I've become very clear that we all have access to hearing *The Voice*—God's highest wisdom for each of us. In this book, I share some of my favorite messages that people from around the world have sent to me, as well as some of Greg's and my own.

The way I look at it, anytime I have a quandary, I can do one of two things: mull the problem over and over in my mind which usually gets me nowhere, or get quiet and listen to the wisdom of *The Voice* within me, knowing it is Divine Intelligence at work in my life. I've learned that I'm much happier if I do the latter, and the more often the better. I started doing CWGs roughly once a week after getting the following message in late 2014, as I was nearing the end of a deep grieving process over moving from Nashville to Los Angeles:

> *Prioritize these CWGs weekly. Then watch the sadness dissipate in your life. This is the best way I can recommend to stay in your good-feeling, clear place. You need look no further than yourself.*

I have each of my CWGs saved into a folder on my laptop, titled with its date and whatever the main topic was. It's fascinating to go back and read them as months and years go by, to see how they've played such an integral part in my life.

My hope is that, as you read and follow the pragmatic suggestions in this book, you will also begin to regularly engage your own inner *Voice*. I further hope you learn to trust it and to act on its guidance for you.

Annie Sims
Los Angeles, California
January 9, 2019

HOW TO GET THE
MOST FROM THIS BOOK

Wisdom that Works is a complete guide to understanding the messages from *Conversations with God* and applying them in your everyday life. It consists of six chapters with four lessons in each. Every lesson is based on a Core Concept from CWG and includes Self-Reflection Questions and Action Steps designed to help you explore that lesson's meaning and implement it in your daily experience. The lessons are in essentially the same form as you would find online in the CWG Online School.

I strongly suggest that you move at the pace of only one lesson per week, in order to allow its message to sink deeply into your consciousness. Each lesson builds upon the previous one, so please be sure to do them in order. If you follow this weekly timetable, it will take you approximately six months to finish the book.

You'll want to compile your answers and experiences into a journal or a folder on your computer or tablet. Or, if you'd like, you can join me in the online school where you can post your responses, and I will give you feedback on your work:

https://www.cwg.foundation/p/WtW

I can also answer any questions that may come up for you about the *Conversations with God* material. Whether you choose to do these lessons on your own or with my assistance, my promise is, if you stick with them to the end, you will find you have a broader perspective, and quite possibly, a happier experience of day-to-day life.

At the end of each lesson's Self-Reflection Questions and Action Steps, I've written a new Postscript which contains additional understandings I've gained since first creating the course. Each Postscript is followed by a communication received from *The Voice* that pertains to that lesson's message. In the interest of anonymity I have chosen to credit each *Voice* quote with only the person's first name and city in which he or she lives. You may, however, readily notice which ones are mine!

As you move through this book you'll likely recognize my passion not only for using Neale's *Conversations with God* material to create a better life, but also for doing my own CWGs so I can hear what *The Voice* would have me know in any given moment. As it wisely told me several years ago:

> *Go Within for guidance. This is the most important thing any/all of you can do.*
> *THIS is what you are here to teach, Annie. That prayer is a two-way communication.*

Chapter 1

THE BASICS

Chapter 1, Lesson #1

Welcome to the first lesson in Chapter 1. Over the next four weeks we will deeply explore "The Basics"—four of the most fundamental concepts that are woven throughout the entire Conversations with God Cosmology.

We'll begin with the single most important message from CWG. If this were the only concept you could fully grasp, it would be enough to change your life and everyone else's around you for the rest of your days.

But first, a little background, if I may . . .

In November 2004, I came home from grocery shopping to find my dear husband Greg as white as a sheet. He was so obviously shaken I immediately exclaimed, "Honey, what's wrong?!" He numbly handed me the phone and said, "Look at the caller ID." When I did, it read "Neale Donald Walsch."

As I stood there with my jaw gaping open, Greg explained that Neale had called to say he'd heard my latest CD (I was writing and recording country music at the time), he loved it and wanted me to tour with him, and would be calling back in a day or two to discuss it! To make a long story short, Greg and I wound up tagging along with Neale on his five-week, eight-country European tour the following year. Little did I know then that this marvelous trip would set the rest of my life's work in motion.

I went on to change musical formats and now mostly write and record songs with

an inspirational message. I lead a *Conversations with God* spiritual study group, I'm a CWG Life Coach, I sing and speak at Unity Churches and Centers for Spiritual Living, and am secretary/treasurer of the Conversations with God Foundation. I am very aware of what a great honor it is to serve in this way. Neale often says, "To whom much has been given, much is asked," and I am most happy and grateful to share with you what I have learned while working at his side for more than a decade.

Annie & Neale at the United Nations in Vienna, Austria.

As I stated earlier, if our first concept is the only one you "grok in fullness," as the author Robert Heinlein used to say—if this is the only concept you really get, and if you apply it in your life—you will find yourself making all manner of choices that inure to your benefit and the benefit of others.

Please notice I said, "if you apply it in your life." I said that for a very specific reason. What good is all this esoteric knowledge if it is not applied and made functional in your day-to-day living? Whenever I introduce a person or an audience to CWG I always tell them, "It doesn't matter if you believe the premise that Neale hears God talking to him. What matters is, do these concepts work to create a better life?"

For me the answer is a resounding "yes!" The phrase that kept coming to mind when starting to write these lessons was "Wisdom that Works." We can talk back and forth all day long about philosophical and spiritual principles, but if you do nothing else as a result of reading this book, my wish for you is that you turn the knowledge you find here into your own wisdom—wisdom that you can *use*.

So let's get started, shall we, with concept #1, the grand-daddy of all CWG concepts—the first Statement of Ultimate Truth from *Conversations with God, Book 1*:

WE ARE ALL ONE.

Okay, okay, we've all heard this a thousand times, right? But what exactly does this expression mean, and what are its implications? I'll share with you some of my thoughts about its meaning, but you get to decide for yourself what its implications are in your own life.

On my Facebook page where it asks us to state a religion, I have these four simple words: "We are all One." I'd say many people think it's just a nice idea, and I used to be one of them. But the more I remember, the more I get that this is meant to be taken literally.

Perhaps nowhere is this illustrated more clearly than in the fascinating book *My Stroke of Insight: A Brain Scientist's Personal Journey* by Dr. Jill Bolte Taylor, a neuroanatomist who had a stroke at age 37. Step-by-step she witnessed the breakdown of her left brain, which is where all of our linear cognitive functioning happens. Although it took her eight years to recover, this may have been the perfect thing to have happened because she learned so much from the experience, and we get to learn from it, too.

I love how the insights that Dr. Taylor gained completely corroborate fundamental CWG concepts, including the idea that we are all One. As her left brain became incapacitated and she was only able to access her right brain, she realized she was separate from nothing, and that all of life is literally connected. With her left brain programming stripped away, she no longer saw her body as having any boundaries.

When looking at her arm she couldn't see where it ended and where the space beside it began, because they are made of the same energy. She intuitively *felt* her connection to everything and said it was the most blissful experience she had ever known.

Also, interestingly, Dr. Taylor could no longer differentiate the spatial relationships of objects she saw. Until someone moved, everything looked flat, as if it were all on one plane.

What we forget is that our brains learned all of that programming of separation when we were babies. In order to make sense of our three-dimensional world and to be able to move through it, we had to learn to think in terms of "here," "there," and "the space in-between." This set us up for a lifetime of feeling separate from everything and from each other. Can you join me now in seeing this illusion for what it is? Can you really "get" that your thought that you are separate from any other part of life is false? And if so, would this knowing cause you to act any differently than you do now?

Please write in your journal or post on the website your answers to the following Self-Reflection Questions:

1. Do you believe you are one with God? If so, have you always known this at a gut level, or did you come to know it later in life? If you don't believe you are one with God, why not? Please explain.

2. Do you believe you are one with all other people, including those you disagree with? Do you believe you are one with those who your government declares are your "enemies"? How about rapists and murderers? If you deeply knew you were one with every single person on the Earth, would you feel or act any differently? If so, how? Please explain.

3. Do you believe you are one with all you see around you—every rock, every tree, every animal, every insect, everything? If you deeply knew you were one with all of life, would you do anything differently? Would you chop down that tree? Would you change what (who) you eat? Would you crush that spider in your house or would you perhaps trap it with a large cup, slide a piece of cardboard under it, and release it outside? Do you think it matters?

4. If the entire population of the Earth believed the concept "We are all One," what changes do you think we would see in the world?

The following are Action Steps for you to take over the next week:

1. Go to the website *TED.com/talks* and search for "My Stroke of Insight." Here you will find Dr. Taylor relating her amazing story in an 18-minute TED talk. There have been over 20 million views. Please watch it, and if you agree that it's "an idea worth spreading," share it with others.

2. Set aside five minutes of quiet time each morning to remember your Oneness with everyone and everything, then set an intention to use this knowingness in all of your encounters as you move through the day. Notice if

this changes your relationship with anyone or anything. If it does, please write about those experiences in your journal, or post them on the website.

◇◇◇

Postscript

Unity. Oneness. A lot of people talk about it. Unity Churches and Centers for Spiritual Living, who teach that we are one with God and each other, continue to gain in popularity worldwide. Humanity's Team's annual Global Oneness Day gets bigger every year. The Global Oneness Project's ongoing aim to unite people around the world is affecting real positive change on our planet.

This concept of Oneness sounds nice, and maybe even idealistic, but what does it really mean, scientifically? In the years since first writing these lessons, I've grown in my awareness that it means there is no place where you stop and I start. There is no place where God ends and we begin. It means there is One Energy Everywhere that pervades everything seen and unseen. It means there is no spot where God is not.

Now, does this mean It doesn't localize Itself? No, It most assuredly does. (You may notice throughout this book that I use the pronoun "It" rather than "He" for God because I believe God is beyond gender.) Oneness is not "sameness." I don't have to give up "me" to be one with you. You and I and all the various physical forms we see are God, having localized and focused Its energy in such a way as to become individuated. It *looks* like It has separated Itself because, in physicality, it appears that we have boundaries. This, however, is an illusion.

Perhaps the biggest issue my online students have had with this lesson is moving beyond *knowing* Oneness conceptually to *experiencing* it in their daily lives. Yet, according to CWG, this is the very reason God chose to differentiate Itself in the first place. God created the Realm of the Physical with its illusion of relativity so It could experience what It knows Itself to be. Ah, there's the challenge! Thankfully, there are a myriad of ways to experience Unity, perhaps none more potent than a simple walk in nature. As we move with heightened awareness in the midst of God's great handiwork, we can say to ourselves, "I am that. I am!"

It's a process, my friends. Deepening our understanding from knowing we are all part of the One to experiencing it is a lifelong journey. Even when we really get it, sometimes life will present us with a challenge that can cause us to forget. And that, of course, is perfect because it gives us a brand new opportunity to remember once again, who we really are.

So onward and upward we go together. In truth, there is no teacher and no student here, as we who present the *Conversations with God* material learn just as much from working with you as you learn from working with us.

As I've heard Neale say many times, "We teach what we have to learn." If you choose to interact with me online, I'm sure you'll have a thing or two (or three or four . . .!) to teach me. We're all in this together because, all together now . . .

We are all One!

THE VOICE

Kim (Waynesville, North Carolina)

I am here today to tell you with complete certainty that you are pure love, your heart is pure, and you are 1000% worthy of ALL you desire. Remind yourself many times a day to breathe and honor yourself, for you are one of my greatest treasures. You are ME and I am you, and I know you know I know!

Sophie (Boulogne, France)

Q: Dear God, please explain to us more about unity.

Dear child, it is all very simple and complex at once, for you are but one body, created from love and light. Think of the sun. It is one great ball of energy and also billions of rays. Think of the rain; think of the grass. In each case there is one basic component being divided into innumerable forms. All looking alike from afar, all different when you get closer, and together creating perfection.

Q: Are you saying perfection is about being united?

In a way it is. Perfection isn't a goal for the soul who knows itself to be so. But it can be for the mind, and the mind believes in disunity. The moment consciousness penetrates the mind and opens it to the reality of unity, a shift occurs and perfection becomes about harmony, cooperation and love.

Life is created from unions.

A conscious being aware of unity changes his habits, his beliefs, leaves fear behind, and starts acting upon love and solely upon love. If hundreds, thousands, or millions of people operated this shift at once, the shift would be monumental and would change everything on your planet. Unity is the way to perfection as you dreamt it, as it is the only way to peace and harmony. As you become aware that you are all One, you can only leave judgment behind and start treating yourself and others better. And so life begins.

Chapter 1, Lesson #2

Last week we began our first lesson by exploring the single most important concept from the entire Conversations with God Cosmology. We looked at the meaning of these four simple words: "We are all One." When we embrace and act on this one basic concept, we can completely change our experience of life on this planet.

In our second lesson, I want to explore what may well be the second most important concept from CWG: the second Statement of Ultimate Truth from *Book 1*. This concept consists of only *two* words, yet when deeply understood and acted upon, it also has the potential to be a big life-changer:

THERE'S ENOUGH.

That's it. There's enough. Hmmm . . . So why is this so important to know? Because the vast majority of people who don't know it are not experiencing the great joy that life is meant to be. Because the vast majority of people think there are limits to the goodness that life is, and they come from that illusion of limitation in their thoughts and actions. And perhaps most importantly, because the thought that there is *not* enough causes us to withhold God's great gifts from each other.

Let's look at what God really is, in order to grasp this idea of non-limitation. God is the joyfully loving process of life force energy, and It is omnipresent. It is in the seen and unseen, particles and waves, matter and anti-matter. It is everything, everywhere!

This life force energy is constantly unfolding and enfolding itself, transforming energy into matter, then moving back into energy. Or as University of London physicist, David Bohm, a protégé of Einstein's, put it, moving from the implicate order to the explicate order, and back again. Moving from what CWG calls the Realm of the Spiritual to the Realm of the Physical or from the Absolute to the Relative, and back again.

This process *never stops*, so how can this energy be limited? It most certainly cannot be, because we know that energy can be neither created nor destroyed . . . it just *is*, and it is ours to manipulate as much as we know we are able! The masters who have walked the earth with this knowledge have shown us how seemingly miraculous this energy trans-mutation can be. I'm reminded of the Biblical story of the loaves and fishes. It looked like Jesus turned nothing into something, but he actually transformed energy into matter. And don't forget, he said: "These things and more you shall do also."

Michael Talbot's fascinating book *The Holographic Universe* gives countless other examples of people in both history and the present day who are able to trans-mutate energy into physicality. How can they do this? Because they know at the deepest level who they are, which is That Without Limitation. They not only allow God to express *through* them, they allow God to express *as* them.

What a wonderful goal to aim for! To really know that we are without limits and to allow ourselves to simply be vessels for this never-ending abundance to express through us and as us.

What would that look like in our lives? What would we give more of to others as a result of this knowingness? More love? More money? More help? More time? More kindness? Simply more of ourselves?

❊❊

Please write in your journal or post on the website your answers to the following Self-Reflection Questions:

Is there anything in your life you think you don't have enough of? If so, what is it and how much would be enough? What would it take for you to think you *do* have enough of it? Please examine your thoughts about this very deeply and write what comes to mind.

The following are Action Steps for you to take over the next week:

Conversations with God says the quickest way to experience that you have enough of something is to be the source of it for another. Here are some ways you can do that:

1. Decide to feel, then express more love to someone in your life, be it a spouse, partner, relative, friend, or even a beloved pet.

2. Decide to give more money away to a person in need or a charity of your choice.

3. Decide to help someone who would benefit from it.

4. Decide to give more of your time to someone who would appreciate spending more time with you.

5. Decide to offer a "random act of kindness" to a stranger.

After taking these five Action Steps, please write in your journal or post on the website a brief summary of what you did in each situation, how you think it affected the other, and how it made you feel.

Postscript

In this Postscript I want to share the story one of my online students posted after doing #5 above, with the hope that it will inspire you to take these Action Steps as well. These are not just stepping stones designed to propel you further on your own spiritual journey; if you do them as directed, they will likely have positive repercussions for those around you, and even beyond. This is because, as *Conversations with God* says, "All true benefits are mutual."

Here's what happened, in her own words, when Cynthia in Atlanta went out on a limb and decided to offer a "random act of kindness" to a stranger:

> I decided to fill up someone's car with gas. I stopped at the first gas station near my coffee shop, but for some reason no one showed up. I decided to pick up my coffee and then stop at the gas station near my house. This gas station has twelve pumps. I stopped at the first pump and waited for a bit but everyone was already filling up their car with gas. Then I decided to drive my car to a different pump and I said to myself, "I'll wait for a minute and see what happens."
>
> Then this beautiful soul parked her car behind mine. I looked at her and smiled. She smiled back. I thought, "That's a good sign. She seems nice." Then I went to her and here's how the conversation went:

> Cynthia: *Hi Ma'am. I know I sound so weird, but can I buy you gas?*

The lady was surprised to see someone by her car so she kind of panicked, then smiled.

Woman: *What? Why?*

Her eyes grew wide.

Cynthia: *I just want to be kind. I'm dedicating this month to kindness.*

Woman: *Are you sure?*

Cynthia: *Yes! I really want to!*

Then the lady brought both of her hands into prayer and looked up to the sky.

Woman: *Thank you, God! Thank you, God!*

And she began crying at the gas station. Then she moved from hugging me to crying, back and forth, so many times.

Woman: *I just called the bank, and I only had ten dollars in my account. I have been helping my mother out because she's sick, and it's been so hard for me financially.*

We kept hugging, crying, and laughing. I was her miracle, and she was mine. She opened my heart and gave more meaning to my life.

The lesson that I shared with people and with myself from this experience was very life-changing. We are *all* messengers of God. Each one of us.

We don't need to look too far to help someone. When we want to help, it can be the person right next to us. What was mind-blowing for me in this experience is that I hesitated *so* many times to stop this act of kindness, and I almost canceled the whole thing. I thought of doing something simpler. But something kept pushing me forward. I couldn't wrap my mind around this. I really couldn't and still can't!

THE VOICE

Allan (Alberta, Canada)

Love is the only thing you need to be. Generosity is what you are most when you call yourself Divine.

Laura (Maitland, Florida)

Q: The way my life is now—the financial struggle—is this the way it's going to be? Is this it? I feel so strongly that the "lack" I experience is holding me back from something far more important.

The prosperity comes from doing that which is so important. This is why it is so important to use your talent and do the work that you are here for. Do it—get moving!

Chapter 1, Lesson #3

Over the past two weeks we've deeply explored the first two Statements of Ultimate Truth from *Conversations with God, Book 1*, the concepts "We are all One" and "There's enough." In this lesson we will look at the third and final concept in the Three Statements of Ultimate Truth.

This is one I've been able to fully implement in my own life and I hope that after digging a little deeper into it, you will, too. It makes for such a joyous way to live!

Some of my friends who know me best call me the "Blond Tornado." This is because I'm a "do-er." With both my husband and me working out of our home, I have to be.

Or do I?

Not really, of course. I'm very clear that every single task and chore I assign myself is just something I'm choosing to do. But if I want our household to be run a certain way—if there is a standard of cleanliness and organization that makes me feel comfortable—then I know it's up to me to do what it takes to make that happen. And when I'm on a roll cleaning the house, and you happen to be standing in my way, watch out!

Have you ever heard the saying, "If you have something that needs doing, give it to a busy person"? Churches and charities probably wouldn't survive without us "busy" people. I was part of a three-woman cat and kitten rescue organization in our rural county outside of Nashville, and we were able to save hundreds of kitties each year. We were busy!

So why do I keep our home running like a well-oiled machine, and why did I spend countless hours nursing, nurturing, and cleaning up after my foster kitties? I know I don't *have* to do any of these things. As our third CWG concept states:

THERE IS NOTHING YOU HAVE TO DO.

It also tells us there is only one reason to do anything: to announce and to declare, to express and to experience, who we decide we are.

I know I am a tidy person who would go crazy living in a disorganized mess of a house, so I keep things put away and reasonably clean. I know I've always been a huge animal lover, and since childhood I've been aware of the over-population of companion animals here in the U.S., so for years I have decided to do something about it. I know I can't save all of them, but I can save some of them.

Did you ever hear the story of the little boy standing on the shoreline amidst hundreds of starfish that had washed up on the beach? He was throwing the starfish back into the sea, one at a time, so they could survive. A "grown-up" passed by and said, "Why, son, you can't save all those starfish. There are just too many of them, so it doesn't matter what you do." The little boy, undeterred, tossed back another starfish and said, "It matters to *this* one."

At the end of the day, it's up to each of us to decide if we're living our day-to-day lives in harmony with our own ideas about who we are. If you don't like something you're doing, now is a good time to stop and think about why you're doing it.

⬦⬦

Please write in your journal or post on the website your answers to the following Self-Reflection Questions:

1. What do you do for a living? Do you love what you do and feel that you're working in your own "right livelihood"? If not, can you think of a way to move into it? What would that look like for you?

2. Name five things you do on a regular basis that allow you to express and experience who you've decided you are, and write out why you do them. For example, "I do _____ because I am ___." ("I do *this* because I am *that*.")

The following is an Action Step for you to take over the next week:
Make a list of everything you're currently doing that doesn't feel in alignment with who you've decided you are. Make a second list of what would be required to change those things. During the next week, see if you can implement those changes, then write in your journal or post on the website how it's working for you.

Postscript

Stop "shoulding" on yourself.

Okay, pun intended, but seriously, can you stop saying, "I should do this," and "I should do that"? I think in these modern times many of us put way too much on ourselves. My best friend in Sweden nearly had a nervous breakdown because she was trying to be all things to all people: good mother, loving wife, keeper of the house, cooker of the meals, taxi service for the kids—and doing all of these things *perfectly* while holding down a demanding forty-hour-per-week job. I was shocked when I saw how haggard my once so young and beautiful friend looked. Just who put these requirements on her? Not to be unkind, because she was just doing her best, but truthfully, *she* did. My friend was "shoulding" on herself all over the place!

Do you find yourself doing this in your day-to-day life? Do you tend to take on more than you can handle? Or do you tell yourself you should do things you don't want to do, simply because of a belief you hold about it? If so, I invite you to question your prior assumption. Ask yourself if it's really true that you should do such a thing. Of course, if it's something you feel you couldn't live happily without doing, then by all means, do it. But if it's something you would live more happily *without* doing, I invite you to consider dropping it.

Please remember this: A belief is just a thought you keep thinking over and over, and a thought is just something you're making up. If you believe you should do a particular thing, look to see where the originating thought behind that belief came from. Did it come from your own mind or from someone else's? Then deeply question the thought. Byron Katie's Four Questions from her book *Loving What Is* would come in handy here:

1. Is it true?

2. Can you absolutely know that it's true?

3. How do you react when you think that thought?

4. Who would you be without the thought?

If you'd be happy, joyous, and free without the thought that you should do that particular thing—whatever it is—give yourself permission to change your mind.

THE VOICE

Greg (Nashville, Tennessee)

Look to see how you feel while you are doing this thing. Do you feel exhilarated and joyous, or do you feel tired and "drudgerous"?

All actions lead you to your goal as long as you hold the vision of it in your mind and soul. For if your mind and soul agree, you will achieve great things in your life. Eliminate those actions that make you feel tired and bored, and you will move along your path more efficiently.

Chapter 1, Lesson #4

We're going to conclude our first chapter with a practical concept you can use every single day. With a little practice you'll find you can use this message at will, whenever you have questions about how to proceed in your life:

GOD IS TALKING TO US ALL THE TIME.

If you have not experienced this in your own life, then I'd really like to help you do that. *Conversations with God* says in *Book 1* that God speaks to us through thoughts, feelings, experiences, and when all else fails, through words. Why "when all else fails, through words"? Because, as we all know, words can sometimes be taken the wrong way. Ever send an email or text to someone who completely misinterpreted your intent? Ouch!

I'd like to share with you some of the ways I experience God talking to me—how I receive communication from my Higher Self, because that's really what we're talking about here. God is our own Higher Self. It's within us, It's all around us, It's who we are, and It's immediately accessible and ready to guide us through each and every moment.

Have you ever experienced a split-second flash of insight? If so, that was God talking to you. It could have been a great idea that popped into your head or a sudden knowing of how to handle a dangerous situation. Or . . . it might have been a very brief feeling of, "Uh-oh, this could be bad." I strongly encourage you to listen if that ever happens to you. One time I ignored a warning flash because it came and went in an instant, and my mind immediately told me the feeling didn't make sense. I'm here to tell ya, ignoring that split-second warning led to one really miserable *year* for me. Now, as we are taught in CWG, life is perfect, and works itself out in the process of life itself, so I came through it all fine in the end. And the point can be made that the warning was simply a "heads up" that I was in for a rough ride that would lead to my spiritual growth. But it only took once for me to learn that I'll never again ignore a split-second warning flash.

There are other ways that God talks to me much more frequently, and one is through a symbol that shows up over and over again. I've heard from many people who also see recurring symbols. For one person it's an infinity sign; for others, it's a pattern of numbers that keeps showing up.

For me, my symbol from Deity is "333." You would not believe how many times over the years I've seen the number "333," and I take it as a sign that I'm on track in my life. I even noticed some time after moving into our house in Nashville that the number "333" was ingrained in the wood on our stairs! I asked God once what this meant and heard these three three-word sentences in my head:

> *I love you.*
> *All is well.*
> *Be at peace.*

At one of Neale's retreats, he mentioned the number "333." I about fell off my chair and shared with him on the break how significant that number is for me. And then later, just to have a little fun, he announced, "At 3:33 this afternoon we'll be having a conversation with God . . ." This was that very first CWG I mentioned in the Introduction, where I gained clarity about animal suffering.

If there's anything Neale and I want you to know, it's that we all can have our own conversations with God. Here's how: If you have a question that's weighing on you, simply write it down on a notepad. Then you can do one of two things. You can either go very deeply within in meditation, or just ponder the question as you're falling asleep at night. Either way, as you come back to wakefulness, often the answer will be in your head in the form of a thought. Get out your pen and notepad and write down whatever comes to you. Don't judge it or try to force it. Just allow the message to flow through you, one word or phrase at a time.

Please don't be discouraged, however, if nothing happens at first. Quieting the mind takes practice, so it gets easier and feels more natural the more you do it. I promise you, if you keep trying, the words will come eventually. If at first you don't "succeed," try, try again!

What I have found when people share their messages with me is this: Although the questions may be specific to their personal situation, the answers that come through are often universal in scope and beneficial for us all.

Here's a P.S. to that previous three-word, three-sentence answer I received when I asked God about the meaning of my "333s." It took me years to realize that the answer I received to my very first question also began with three three-word sentences:

> *Just BE happy.*
> *Trust the process.*
> *Go on faith.*

Wow. I love it when I see my "333s"! I stop and drink in the moment every single time.

After I discovered how easy it is to have these written conversations, I found another way to receive quick answers to small decisions. A Reiki practitioner friend, Gaia Tossing, showed me that we can ask God to speak to us through our body in the form of "yes" or "no" answers to questions. I started calling this the "God Within Us" process. Here's how to do it:

Stand with your hand parallel to the top of your head (palm facing downward) and ask God to show you your "yes" answer. Then somewhat slowly move your hand down from the top of your head, down in front of your face, neck, chest, torso, and then hold it in front of your abdomen. Keep your palm close to your body while doing this so that it's close to your chakras or energy centers. When your hand stops in front of your tummy, see if you feel your body pulled forward or backward. This will be your "yes" answer. (I've learned that the direction of the movement can vary from person to person.) Then repeat the process, asking God to show you your "no" answer. Your body will be pulled in the opposite direction.

Once you know your "yes" and "no" answers and you relax into trusting this process, you will always have quick access to your Higher Self and can ask It what is in your highest and best interest regarding any decision. I use this to test which vitamins and supplements to take by holding the pill in my hand while moving it down my body. When I get a "yes" pull, I know the supplement is good for me that day. If I get a "no" pull, I don't take it. I'm actually at the point now where I don't really need to do the process. As soon as I ask, I know the answer. If I double check what I hear in my head, it's always corroborated by the process.

Some people use a pendulum in the same way. If it does a circular swing in one direction it's a "yes." If it swings the other way, it's a "no." Others do muscle testing with their chiropractor or other alternative healer. These processes may seem strange or even spooky at first, but there's a very good reason they work: God is communicating with us all the time and is closer than our own hands and feet. It is everywhere present and It knows all.

Our soul is the part of us that is purely connected to God, so it has access to all of Its information. Our mind's perspective is very limited, and that's why it's in our best interest to use both the mind *and* the soul, as Neale's book *When Everything Changes, Change Everything* tells us.

There's one caveat to this lesson's concept, however: Our left brain can sometimes get into a thought pattern that is detrimental, and this is *not* God talking to us. (Yes, I know, God is all there is, so I'm asking you to trust that this is an example of a "Divine Dichotomy," two apparently contradictory truths co-existing!) When you hear your mind running loops of self-berating thoughts, worries, or doubts, this is just monkey-mind chatter. How can we tell the difference? As *Book 1* says on page 5, "The Highest Thought is always that which contains joy. The Clearest Words are those words which contain truth. The Grandest Feeling is that feeling which you call love."

Joy, truth, love. Simple, huh?!

Please write in your journal or post on the website your answers to the following Self-Reflection Questions:

1. Do you feel that God has communicated with you before? If so, is this a common occurrence or a rare one?

2. If you don't feel that God has communicated with you before, do you believe it is possible? Do you believe you are worthy of receiving direct communication from God?

3. Do you have a recurring symbol that appears in your life? If so, please write about what your experience has been with that and what it means to you.

The following are Action Steps for you to take over the next week:

1. Practice doing the "God Within Us" process.

Ask God for answers to different kinds of queries. For example, try holding different food items while doing the process and asking if they are beneficial to your body. You might ask this: "Dear God, is it in my highest and best interest to_____?"

Then see which way you are pulled. If you feel good about doing so, use the answers you receive, and see if they help you. Start with little things, not major life decisions. Don't file for a divorce simply because you get a "yes" answer! Big decisions require deep contemplation and connection with the Divine.

Note: If you already are comfortable using a pendulum, muscle testing, or something similar, just use that. There are probably infinitely different ways to use the "God Within Us" process. Just do whatever works for you.

2. At least three times over the next week, write down a question on your
   notepad either before meditating or retiring at night. When you come
   back to wakefulness, write down what comes to you.

After taking these Action Steps, please write in your journal or post on the website a
brief summary of what you did in each situation, and how it worked for you.

Postscript

Greg and I continue to see our "333s." One of the most magnificent examples involved
recurring signs about a song we recorded in my country music days, "80 Acres of Stars."
On our UK tours, it had always been everyone's favorite, so we knew we wanted to
put it on my next CD. He and I were amazed when the digital time stamp was—you
guessed it—3:33. With absolutely no intention on our part, the length of the recording
was exactly three minutes and thirty-three seconds. Then, when I traveled with my publi-
cist on a radio tour to promote the single, it seemed crazy, but we kept crossing Highway
333, over and over again.

Fast forward to 2013, when Greg and I took a weekend to drive up the Pacific Coast
Highway in Southern Oregon. He had to slam on the brakes when he noticed a huge sign
that said, "80 Acres Road." We've never before or since seen a road by that name. Now,
here's the real kicker: When we looked across the highway from 80 Acres Road, we were
dumbfounded to see the PCH mile marker 333. I kid you not, and I have a photograph
to prove it! I must admit we're still wondering: What was the message here? As far as we

Annie under the "80 Acres Road" sign on the Pacific Coast Highway, across from mile marker 333.

know, the single ran its course a long time ago. It was our most successful endeavor, garnering a great review and DisCovery Award from Music Row Magazine, the music video was broadcast on CMT's Pure Country, and the song stayed on Music Choice Americana's Top Ten list for three months. But could it perhaps be as my friends Jan Garrett and JD Martin say in their song title, "It Ain't Over Yet"?! The recording and video of "80 Acres of Stars" are still out there on YouTube and iTunes. As Jan's and JD's lyrics say, "You just don't know, ya never know . . ."

Post-Postscript

In the summer of 2016, I was feeling down-hearted about the seemingly long time it was taking for Greg to become firmly established as a composer in Hollywood. We took a day to go outside and play, knowing this is vital to keeping us in our good-feeling place. We drove our Volkswagen, "The Happy Camper," to our favorite beach in Malibu, Point Dume, popped the top, and climbed the point to enjoy the views. I then decided to take an afternoon nap, and on the way back to the camper, I noticed two license plates, the first of which had the number "333" on it. As we've gotten quite used to seeing our lucky number, I pointed it out to Greg, but didn't think too much of it until we passed another car, this one displaying the number "3333" on its license plate. Wow. This really gave me pause. I knew it was a message that everything was okay. I drifted peacefully off to sleep, comforted by the sound of the breaking waves and the positive messages I'd just received.

Upon awakening from my nap, I asked God while I was still in the alpha state, "What is the significance of the '333' and '3333'?" I heard this:

The veil is thinning.

I'd never heard this expression before, but I figured it meant the veil between the physical and spiritual realms. I further heard these four 3-word sentences:

Keep the faith.
Work toward knowing.
Go the distance.
You're almost there.

Please remember, I'd just seen *four* 3s on the second license plate!

Two months later, Greg and I decided to subscribe to Gaia TV and were looking for something interesting to watch. We happened upon an episode of George Noory's *Beyond Belief* in which he was interviewing a filmmaker named Richard Martini. I had to grab the remote and rewind the program when Richard said his wife had heard the following response from a departed loved one via a medium, when she asked why he was coming through so strongly:

The veil is thinning.

Another month went by. Greg and I were camping at the Grand Canyon, again to re-center ourselves in preparation for another chunk of time in hectic Los Angeles. We'd been reading perhaps the most comprehensive book that bridges science and spirituality, *The Source Field Investigations*, by David Wilcock. Greg read a passage to me that also mentioned "a thinning of the veil."

Hmmm . . . Good things come in 3s!

THE VOICE

Donna (Torrance, California)

On the morning of February 24, 2012, I was traveling by plane to Montgomery, Alabama. I was an Enrollment Counselor who assisted in helping children get into college. Weekly, I traveled to different states to accomplish this mission. On that morning shortly after the plane took off, I felt like someone had attached a suction cup to my left arm and was sucking the life out of me. I knew something was going haywire, and I thought I should call the airline stewardess. This little *Voice* whispered:

You are closer to God. Call on Me.

Because I had read Neale Donald Walsch's *Conversations with God* books, I chose to listen, and immediately went into prayer mode asking for God's guidance and direction through this experience. After the prayer, I went immediately to sleep. Note, this was highly unusual because previously, I always found it difficult to sleep on planes and would bring a DVD or book to accompany me during flight. However, this time I went immediately to sleep and woke up when the plane landed.

Upon landing in Dallas, Texas, I went to get my luggage from the overhead compartment but could not pull it down and had to get help. I knew for sure something had gone awry. I met my employee at our connection to continue to our final destination, Montgomery. I explained to the employee what I had experienced in flight and told him that when we arrived in Montgomery I was going to go to the hospital and get checked out. During this conversation, a man sitting behind me tapped me on the shoulder and said, "You cannot get on that plane." In my head I said, "Well, who are you?" He told me that he was a medical doctor and that I should not get on the flight because if I went back into the air I would be subjecting my body to trauma due to the lack of oxygen and the air pressure. He said that even if I made it to Montgomery okay, the hospitals there were so awful they would kill me.

While I processed this information, the doctor immediately took out his phone and dialed 911 and had me picked up by ambulance and driven to the top stroke facility in Dallas. When I arrived at the hospital, I was told by the doctors that I had experienced a miracle because not too many people survive a stroke on a plane and live to tell about it. The doctors kept asking me what I did on the flight. I told them I'd had a conversation with God.

Akiko (Melbourne, Australia)

There was the time I was having a challenge finding a job. I hired my own career consultant, registered with different recruitment agents, met people asking for opportunities, and applied for the roles on the different job boards. Nothing seemed to work. When I thought I'd totally lost physical and emotional energy and I was unable to think what I could do next, I shouted at my Higher Self, "You are not helping me here at all! I'm stuck. I just can't keep going like this. What's the purpose of me experiencing this?" When I was complaining to the Universe, I happened to sit in front of my TV and an Australian football game started. I didn't know why I was sitting there because I wasn't interested in Aussie football at all. When both teams came out to the ground, I saw a huge banner between the teams that said:

We can achieve our goals together. We'll move to the next level.

I couldn't believe what I just saw, but I believed that was the answer to me from God.

The message on the banner was correct. I was offered a position a few weeks later. It was an awesome role in that I could re-create myself anew in the next grandest version of the greatest vision about who I was at that point of my life.

Audrey (Sausset-les-Pins, France)

Q: Hello, I am not sure how to start this dialogue as this is my very first time.

Do as you feel. I am here.

Q: Firstly, I would like to be your friend, and I would like you to be my friend. Are you okay with this?

Everything is okay to Me. I am honored by your friendship.

Q: You're kidding. I am the one who is honored! Is it a reality? Am I really talking to God, and becoming his/her friend?

Yes, and we have been communicating for a long time, and this is just a new way of doing it! Yes, we are becoming friends if you allow it to happen. This is a good start. Remain connected to Me and avoid taking refuge in your mind. Of course you need your mind to write; just be with Me simultaneously.

Chapter 2

CREATION & PURPOSE

Chapter 2, Lesson #1

Welcome to the first lesson in Chapter 2. Together we will explore several CWG concepts pertaining to "Creation and Purpose," and hopefully at the end of the next four weeks you will have more clarity regarding your own power to create and your own life purpose.

But let's be clear here: When I speak about "creating" what I really mean is "calling forth into our experience." Every single thing that can possibly be created has been created already. You may be familiar with the Biblical quote from Isaiah, "Even before you ask I will have answered." In Ultimate Reality there is no such thing as time, and everything exists already. Our job is to align ourselves with our soul's desires and allow what we have called forth to be made manifest in our reality.

Years ago when I was first learning about the Law of Attraction, I was at a Chinese restaurant with a friend who was also trying to figure out how to use this powerful law. After dinner we got our fortune cookies, and mine had a message inside that said, "With our thoughts we create our world." We were amazed because fortune cookies usually contain trite little messages that we share with our friends, have a chuckle over, then discard without a second thought. I still have this one on my vision board, and it brings me to today's concept:

YOU ARE THE CREATOR OF YOUR OWN REALITY.

When most people hear this, as did my friend and I, they think it means we create our external conditions and circumstances, and in part, that's true. But many people who have tried to use the Law of Attraction and found that it "didn't work" for them, have decided the law isn't true. I don't agree. It isn't that the Law of Attraction, which according to Abraham-Hicks states, "That which is like unto itself is drawn," isn't true.

Just look around in nature to see it at work in flocks of birds, bee hives, ant hills, etc. (For Neale's thoughts on the Law of Attraction, please see his chapter titled "The Process of Personal Creation" in *Happier Than God*.)

The reason this law doesn't always work in bringing to us the focus of our desires when we truly believe we can have them is because we're co-creating with others. And because others' desires and beliefs come into play, we don't have total control of our outer world. We do, however, have total control of our inner world—and our inner world is what creates our reality. This is a big difference, and it bears repeating:

OUR INNER WORLD CREATES OUR REALITY.

This is why some people are able to overcome unbelievably difficult situations with amazing grace. People such as Viktor Frankl, who was able to find beauty in what everyone else around him perceived as sheer ugliness and horror in the Nazi concentration camps. People such as Nelson Mandela, who was able to maintain his inner peace during 27 long years of imprisonment in South Africa. Their reality was not about the external circumstances they were facing. Rather, it was about who they were being no matter what was going on around them.

Who we are being creates our reality, and this is something we get to choose. Beingness is a choice. At any moment we get to decide who we're going to be regarding any event or situation.

This is where Neale's powerful book, *When Everything Changes, Change Everything* (WECCE), comes into play. It states that there are three types of realities:

Distorted Reality
Observed Reality
Ultimate Reality

I believe that Viktor Frankl and Nelson Mandela were able to stay for the most part in Observed and Ultimate Reality during their incarcerations. That's how they were able to remain grounded in love no matter what was going on. And the key to staying in their God-space? Not judging the conditions. They simply *observed* their world around them without judgment—as much as possible, anyway.

WECCE says when we judge conditions based on our prior data about that type of condition, it's very easy to jump to Imagined Truth. In other words, we tend to let our imaginations run away with us and we believe the Imagined Truth is real. This is what leads to a Distorted Reality. If Frankl and Mandela had done that, it's likely they would have never made it out alive.

When we see what is apparently so, or what WECCE calls Apparent Truth, then we can move up to Observed Reality. This is preferable to Distorted Reality because we are not making judgments about what is going on. We are simply observing what is happening.

We can move to a higher reality still, Ultimate Reality, by moving to the Actual Truth. Just what is the Actual Truth about any given situation? The Actual Truth is what your soul knows about it, which is infinitely more than your mind does. The mind *thinks* it knows everything, but its data is extremely limited. It is a very useful tool, of course, so WECCE advocates using what it calls the "Mechanics of the Mind" and the "System of the Soul" together.

So what does all of this have to do with creating your reality? It's simple, really:

You can look at the world with skewed thoughts about it and your reality will be distorted.

You can look at the world, witnessing only what you see without making judgments about it, and your reality will be simply that: observed.

Or you can look at the world observing what is so *and* allowing your Higher Self/God to communicate with you about it, to arrive at Ultimate Reality. Wouldn't that be a great place to not only arrive *at*, but to come *from* in our day-to-day lives?! Those who do this radiate great joy and inner peace that is evident and sometimes contagious! We've all seen people like this, who light up a room the second they walk into it. And people and pets are naturally drawn to them like bees to flowers.

Wanna know something? I've felt that way sometimes. Everywhere I go I make both human and animal friends. And I've been told by a few people that they see light radiating from me. Now, I don't see light around anybody, but it sure was nice to hear that others see it in me!

I like this reality I've created. I *love* this reality I've created. And I thank God for it every day, many times. The words to a clever country song come to mind:

"I like it. I love it. I want some more of it!"

Please write in your journal or post on the website your answers to the following Self-Reflection Questions:

Think of three times you jumped to conclusions about an event. In each scenario, how did you come to realize you had made up an Imagined Truth and a Distorted Reality about it? What, if anything, did you learn from these events?

The following are Action Steps for you to take over the next week:

1. Every day as much as possible, pay attention to any "gut feelings" you have. *Conversations with God* says feelings are the language of the soul (unlike emotions, which come from the mind's thoughts). They are how God communicates with us, offering us guidance and clarity. When you are feeling good (happy, excited, peaceful, etc.), stop and notice the

thoughts you're having that are causing you to feel the positive emotion. When you are feeling bad (worried, angry, frustrated, etc.), stop and
notice the thoughts you're having that are causing you to feel the negative
emotion. (Please note: Emotions are really neither positive nor negative
as they all serve an important purpose, but I use these examples to make
a larger point.) Keep a notepad handy and jot down these observations,
then add them to your journal or post them on the website.

2. When you have a negative emotion, try to trace its origin. Then look to see
   if your thought about what is bothering you is really true, or if your mind
   made an assumption about it, causing you to have an Imagined Truth and
   Distorted Reality about it. Then look for a turn-around thought. Notice
   what is observably true, then ask God in quiet meditation to help you get
   to your Actual Truth about it.

3. Notice also if you have any negative thought patterns that keep repeating
   over and over in your mind, and if so, look to see if they are serving you.
   If they aren't, and they only make you feel bad, decide to stop thinking
   about them. Choose to replace those habits of thought with something
   else that feels better to you. When the old thoughts come up again (and
   they probably will for awhile) simply stop and say, "Thank you for sharing,
   but I'm through thinking about this." And again, think about something
   else. If you do this every time, the thoughts will eventually stop coming up
   for you.

4. Please write about your experiences with #2 and #3 above, and what, if anything, you've gained from taking these steps.

Postscript

Thought for the day (yes, irony noted!): A thought has no basis in fact. Please ponder that for a moment. I'll repeat it here for emphasis:

A THOUGHT HAS NO BASIS IN FACT.

If we think about where thoughts come from, our mind (or someone else's), we realize we're making everything up! Facts and thoughts are two different things.

Remember what I asked you to remember about beliefs in Chapter 1, Lesson #3?

A BELIEF IS JUST A THOUGHT YOU KEEP THINKING OVER AND OVER.

Regarding the Chinese fortune cookie message I told you about earlier in this lesson, "With our thoughts we create our world": If we plug in the ideas above, the larger meaning is, we are creating our reality by the thoughts we hold in mind—the thoughts we believe—that often have no basis in fact.

I recently had a CWG Life Coaching session with a client who moved from South America to the United States eight months ago with her husband and two small children.

She was terrified that they wouldn't be able to make enough money here to survive. They are waiting for her husband's "green card" so he can get a job in his chosen profession, but someone had told them that even then, he would only be able to earn $5,000 per month. She said that wouldn't be nearly enough for their monthly budget of $8,000. She mentioned her fear of not having enough money to pay bills next month, which can, of course, be very scary in a foreign country with a family. I asked her if they have any savings, and she said yes. When I asked her how much, she told me they have $200,000. I exclaimed, "Two hundred thousand dollars?! I would have been concerned if you told me you only have *two* thousand dollars, but you have a hundred times that!"

This tipped me off to the idea that there was more going on here than meets the eye. As she has been a Kabbalist spiritual mentor for five years, I asked her if she had felt divinely guided to move here, and she said yes. I asked, "Did you feel elated when you first moved here?" Again, she said yes. So I asked her, "Do you remember when you first started having this frightened feeling? When did you change from feeling very happy to feeling frightened?" It was, indeed, several weeks prior when that someone had said her husband wouldn't be able to make the kind of income they'd hoped for. She added that it had hit her so hard, she'd retreated to her bed for a week and had felt depressed ever since. Her sadness was so deep, I could hear it in her voice. I told her I suspected she was also feeling a bit homesick, and she immediately admitted she was feeling *very* homesick. I pointed out that this was probably a large part of why she was so sad. Huge changes in our lives, even when we instigate them and are excited about them, can be accompanied by grief. I shared with her that I had gone through major bouts of sadness when I moved from Nashville to Los Angeles, but that it gets better. Once we recognize we are grieving, and we allow ourselves to express it, we can get it out of our system and start moving again toward our soul purpose.

The next step was to point out to her that these thoughts she'd been believing had no basis in fact: "My husband is only going to earn $5,000 per month and that isn't enough to live on. We're going to plow through all of our savings and fail here in the United States." I worked with her to find some positive ideas to replace the negative ones. For example, when we talked about other ways they might make money, she divulged that they are in the process of flipping a house which will likely profit them $30,000. She is also certainly employable, as she is already a U.S. citizen. I said to her, "Wealth is ideas. The possible revenue streams are endless."

She just wasn't seeing them because her deep sadness and fear had knocked her out of alignment so much, she was dwelling totally in her mind, cut her off from her inspired ideas. This brings up a very important point I've made before:

THOUGHTS COME FROM OUR MIND.

Our mind, as we learned in the lesson above, holds extremely limited data. It works much like a computer when confronted with a new situation. It immediately searches its databank for similar situations, analyzes them, then spits out new thoughts—often over-protective ones—because one of the mind's main jobs is to keep the body alive. For that reason, it will tend to offer thoughts that hold us back from doing anything courageous, in its attempts to keep us safe.

So if thoughts come from our mind and they have no basis in fact, what, then, *can* we believe?! We must dig a little deeper to get to our truth about anything:

ACTUAL TRUTH COMES FROM OUR SOUL.

This is because our soul is that part of us that is always purely connected to God. We want to be very careful whether we embrace our mind's thoughts or our soul's truths.

So how do you know the difference? Fortunately, it's easy! When you are feeling great—as my client was, for the first seven months she was here—you are holding the highest truths about yourself and life. If you find yourself starting to feel bad, as she had a few weeks prior, you can rest assured you're starting to believe some thoughts that have no basis in fact.

This is because God is always joyful, loving, accepting, blessing, and grateful, and these are our natural states of being as well. When we are feeling anything less than these Five Attitudes of God, as *Conversations with God* calls them, we have stepped off the path of least resistance, and things start to go sour for us.

What then, to do? As I did with her, try to trace it back to when you last felt happy, and when you started feeling fearful or sad about something. Try to find the "trigger thought" that pulled you off track. Once you find it, examine it very closely to see if you can find any Actual Truth in it.

Chances are, you won't. You can then begin to dismantle the illusion you've created around it and start looking for higher truths about yourself and the situation.

It really helps to remember that God's always got your back. The Universe is constantly conspiring in your favor, even when it doesn't look like it. We didn't come into this world to fail, and failure is just an illusory thought that has no basis in fact anyway. We are all divinely supported, and when we believe *this*, we can move into the real reason we came here in the first place, and fulfill our soul's purpose. We can turn our grandest concept of ourselves into our greatest experience, any way we choose, and we can feel great doing it! More of that, please.

THE VOICE

Ross (San Francisco, California)

Each individuation is a unique set of self-created experiences on the tapestry of life.

Greg (Los Angeles, California)

Q: What about Abraham-Hicks' "17-second Law"?

Exciting, isn't it? This is simply how long it takes for the human brain to rewire enough neurons to line up a different belief. That is why old beliefs are so persistent. They are literally hard-wired into physicality. You are simply creating a new software program to run. (Actually, downloading new firmware would be a more accurate analogy.) Reprogramming is accomplished by meditation (erasure), visioning (development), and replacing old thoughts with new affirmative ones (installation/installing the new program). You can build and run virtually any "software program" that you can create. Everyone is doing this, but most do not do it consciously. Knowing that reality is manifesting through and not to or against you is another key to unlocking this innate creative power.

First, you begin being the New You. The new beliefs aggregate organically over time and the old paradigms disappear gradually. This process of life experience is a journey for most; an overnight transformation for a very few.

Q: Great! So how do we speed the process up? Or would this be less rewarding? To continue our computer analogy, how do we install more RAM?

Nice analogy. Your RAM is your container of consciousness. The more capacity it has, the more space for abundance to flow in to fill the vacuum of your expanded consciousness. Meditating, visioning, and "becoming in advance" are all ways to increase your RAM.

Q: Are there others?

1. *Raising your vibration (doing things you love/fun activities)*

2. *Taking actions that reinforce your new beliefs (what Mary Morrissey calls "sourced actions")*

3. *Being love, giving love*

4. *Blessing everything and everyone*

5. *Focusing on the New You*

6. *Cultivating a feeling of gratitude for all things and all results*

Also, you can add more programmers. These are your co-creators who are drawn to you because of your vibrational match to each other.

Imagine (see it)

Rewire (become it)

Recruit (expand it)

Stay excited about the process, and have fun. That's the whole point!

Chapter 2, Lesson #2

The concept we're going to examine in today's lesson may well be the most useful of all because, more than any other, it can help us realize our life's dream and our soul's purpose:

THE THREE TOOLS OF CREATION ARE:
THOUGHT, WORD, AND ACTION.

If any of you saw Oprah Winfrey's final television show before she signed off after 25 years, you heard her say she believes everyone has a "calling." I think she's right. She has obviously learned a great deal from the countless guests on her show, including many New Thought authors and teachers, and you don't get from where she started to where she is now without some higher purpose at work. Oprah knew she had a calling to teach, but in a much larger way than just the classroom, and teach she did on that final show.

I was reliably informed several years ago that Oprah read *Conversations with God* and liked it very much. It was evident in her talk on that final day because its messages were woven all through it. Time after time during that show, my husband Greg and I looked at each other and said, "That came right out of CWG!"

Greg had a special interest in watching Oprah's last episode because he wrote and produced music for her show the last seven years it was on the air. Matter of fact, it was the performance royalties he received from its worldwide broadcasts that allowed us to move from Orlando to Nashville, and they kept us afloat while creating a new life there during a difficult economic recession. Knowing that this chapter of our lives was about to come to a close, we wanted to be sure to catch her final show to honor what she had done for us.

Greg's calling has always been to be a film composer, and he was told by a very intuitive woman once, "This is what you came here to do." Not a small life's dream, by any means. Getting there has taken the two of us on an extraordinary journey, and hopefully by sharing some of the things he did that worked and some things that didn't work, you will also find a way to realize your own life's dream.

First of all, if you don't know what your calling is, I invite you to be open to higher guidance on this. Your soul knows what makes it leap with joy and what it is passionate about. You need only pay attention to your feelings. I'm not saying there's one thing God wants you to do, and you have to figure it out. I'm saying there must be something you love doing so much you would do it for free, and to actually make your living at it would be a dream come true!

As I was saying, Greg has known since he was a child that he wanted to compose musical scores for movies. But how in the world does a little boy from the mountains of upper East Tennessee get to do that?! Well, creating anything starts with a thought, and his thought was, "This is what I want, so I'm going to do something about it." He took piano lessons for sixteen years, he played saxophone and clarinet in the band, he studied violin, and he went to University and earned a Bachelor of Music degree with Highest Honors. Yet this was before most colleges and universities offered training in film scoring, so now what?

As many of us who graduated with music degrees did, we gigged for a living for a long time. And eventually, Greg landed the fabulous job of writing cues for one of the most successful shows ever on television, *The Oprah Winfrey Show*. Yet, as grateful as he was, the thought persisted in the back of his mind: "I want to be a *film* composer, I want to be a *film* composer . . .!"

This is where things started not working for him. Greg was so *wanting* to score films, he was getting just that in his experience—more wanting to score films! Remember, the Law of Attraction states, "That which is like unto itself is drawn," so his thoughts of wanting to score films were drawing that exact experience to him.

This felt terrible. When he would read about a successful film composer, his stomach would tie up in knots because he wasn't getting to do it yet. His soul was telling him big-time, "You want to be doing this, and you want it so badly it hurts." His thoughts were focused not only on the fact that it hadn't happened yet, but he was also spiraling downward into thoughts like, "So many people want to do this these days, what makes me think I can do it as well as them? I don't even live in LA where all the movies are being made, so how am I going to connect with people in films?" You know, just stinkin' thinkin' stuff.

Well, folks, we are here to tell ya that if you're doing a lot of stinkin' thinkin', you're gonna get whatever you're stinkin' thinkin' about!

I am so grateful we were guided to *Conversations with God* because, before reading these books, we knew nothing about how powerfully creative our thoughts, words, and actions are.

The first thing Greg needed to do was work to clear up his thought process—the first tool of creation. He had to learn to overcome doubts and fears that he wouldn't get to realize his dream, and he had to quit worrying about *how* he was going to do it. I wrote a little limerick that we kept on the fridge that said:

> Mine is not to question how;
> Rather, simply, to allow.
> Maintain always an attitude
> Of never-ending gratitude
> In each blessed moment of now.

Feelings of heartfelt gratitude and appreciation are very magnetizing. They actually cause the Universe to reflect back even more to be grateful for!

So what next? The second tool of creation came into play: Speak your word. Although it felt a bit like stretching the truth at first, when asked on questionnaires what his occupation was, Greg started writing "Film and Television Composer." Then when people started asking him what he does for a living, he would say it *out loud*. Very powerful stuff, here, folks, speaking your word. This energy is more dense than thought energy, so it attracts on a larger level. And when you tell others what it is you intend to do, not only do they add their energy to your vision, they may have ideas and connections to help you make it happen.

A word of caution here: There may be a few nay-sayers (especially family and friends who have known you for a long time) who will say, "You shouldn't do that," or even worse, "*You can't do that*." Please, please, don't listen to them. Rather, choose to spend your time with people who understand how the Universe works and who believe in you.

Finally, the third and most energetically powerful tool of creation gave Greg an opportunity to do what he said he did for a living. He was asked to score a very sweet animated movie starring the voice talents of Jim Belushi and the comedian, Carrot Top, about—get this—*realizing your dreams*. The motto of the film is, "Dreams are powerful things." How perfect is that! And it didn't matter one iota that Greg didn't live in LA. In fact, if he had, he never would have gotten *this* movie, which was, of course, the perfect opportunity to show himself and the rest of the world that he really could create a magnificent underscore for a feature film.

This brings up an important point. We can know in our heart what our calling is, but we may not know if we can really "cut it" . . . until we do. Greg has said many times that this first movie allowed him to know he could compose, arrange, orchestrate, and produce a first-rate score, and that knowingness became a new first tool of creation. His new thought about it became, "Yes, I am really good at film scoring. I am now confident in my ability to offer this service to others."

And about the word "service," let's be honest here. It is a great gift that Greg is giving movie directors and producers because his music is truly exceptional. He has now scored over a dozen films, and a number of people, including critics, say his music is the best thing about some of these movies! None of them would have been served by a mediocre score, so by following his calling, Greg has been a huge blessing to everyone involved. This is not to say that these films didn't present some difficult challenges. They certainly did, but by staying in his knowing that everything would work out perfectly in the end, that is exactly what happened.

It's interesting that his first three movies came about before we ever considered moving to LA. That is how truly powerfully creative our thoughts, words, and actions are.

So it all begins with a thought. However, if you, like Greg, have a really big dream, please be patient. It can take the Universe a little while sometimes to bring all the elements together to make it happen. But remember, all you have to say is "what" and let God take care of the "how." Take for granted that when you follow your heart's desire, it is God's great pleasure to give you the kingdom. Don't strive too hard to make things happen. Rather, take action when you feel inspired to. This may require you to close some doors so that others may open. Do away with what no longer serves you, so that you can focus fully on your goal. As Michael Bernard Beckwith says, "Energy goes where attention flows."

Then, as you move forward toward achieving your goal, remember that life is working itself out in your favor, even when you can't see it yet. Stay in your excitement, joy, and gratitude, then watch the miracles start rolling in. Life is good!

Please write in your journal or post on the website your answers to the following Self-Reflection Questions:

1. Do you feel you have a calling or life's dream? If so, please write about what it is.

2. If you don't feel you have a calling, please take some time to get in touch with what makes you feel really happy or what you are most passionate about, and see if you can find a way to incorporate more of that into your

life. But please don't feel bad if you think you don't have a calling, or you don't know what it is. Just begin to be aware that there may be something inside you that wants to expand and express itself. Then stay open to your Highest Wisdom, which is guiding you always. Please write down any experiences you have during this process. Also, keep in mind that your calling doesn't have to be a paying job. It may be a hobby or volunteer work that you do in your spare time, and it may even cost you money. Because prosperity follows passion, though, it may eventually turn into your livelihood, at least part-time.

3. Where are you on the path to realizing your calling? Are you still in the thinking stage? Have you spoken of it to others? Have you done anything about it? Are you just getting started, mid-way through the process, or is your dream fully realized? How does that feel for you?

4. Please write your thoughts about your calling, whether positive or negative, or both. If you have negative thoughts about whether it will happen, deeply examine whether those thoughts are absolutely true. Then write some better-feeling thoughts that change those negative worries and doubts into positive possibilities.

5. Fill in the blank below about your life's dream, even if it hasn't happened yet: "I am a _____."

If you don't already call yourself what it is you want to do, begin doing that. Speak your word into existence in regard to your calling, and allow yourself to really believe it!

The following is an Action Step for you to take over the next week:

Think of three things you can actively do to help you realize your life's dream, then begin to implement them. Please write in your journal or post on the website how that is working for you.

Postscript

Everything is created twice. Every single thing, be it man-made or God-made, is first a thought before it is a thing. The chair you are sitting in, whether simple or elaborate, was first conceived in someone's mind before it was built. The car you drive is the culmination of many thoughts by many different people working together to cause it to come to fruition. The yellow daffodils of spring were first an idea in the mind of God before they poked through the cold ground. We, ourselves, were created in the mind of God before we were created in the flesh. This omniscient, omnipotent *Voice* said, "Let there be . . ." and it was so. This is the power of the word, and we, like God, get to use it however we see fit.

Since our thoughts, words, and actions lead to our next experience, our invitation from life is to choose them wisely! One of my favorite affirmations is this:

"I listen to the wisdom of *The Voice* within me, knowing it is Divine Intelligence at work in my life. I trust it and I act on it."

A word to the wise, though: Your Higher Self will sometimes lead you into uncharted territory which can be quite challenging and even a bit scary. Because of this, I keep two engraved rocks close at hand to remind me to stay in my knowing that all is well. One says "TRUST." The other says "SMILE."

When I first wrote this lesson for the online school, Greg and I lived in Nashville and he had scored two feature films. We felt very fortunate, considering he had zero Hollywood connections at the time! We were going on faith, trusting *The Voice* to guide and the Universe to provide. A year or so later, the messages we received led us to move to Los Angeles, and much to our surprise, we both love it here! I can't say the process was easy, though. It necessitated renting a guest house for six months to try it out, flying home every few weeks to be with the cats, going way out on a limb financially, etc.

When we found a darling bungalow where we could live with the cats, I knew it was time to sell our beloved dream house in Nashville, which was very, very difficult for me. I grieved greatly over leaving that house, my family, friends, and favorite city behind. I had thought it was going to be home for the rest of my life, but every single CWG I did corroborated that the move was not only in Greg's highest and best interest, it was in mine, too. And even though my Higher Self led me down some rocky roads, it never steered me wrong. The roads are rocky for a reason—to cause us to grow into more than we ever dreamed possible.

One of my favorite quotes from *Conversations with God* is, "Life begins at the end of your comfort zone." When we are willing to take a leap of faith and follow our largest ideas about ourselves as we are guided, our lives begin to really take off. At the end of it all, when I lay my head on the pillow for the last time, I want to look back with a great big smile and say, "I did it! It wasn't always easy, but I wouldn't change a thing. I want to do it all over again!"

A couple of years ago I added to the limerick I quoted in the lesson above. Here is the poem now in its entirety:

Mine is not to question how;
Rather, simply, to allow.
Maintain always an attitude
Of never-ending gratitude
In each blessed moment of now.

Mine is not to question when;
Rather, simply, to begin.
Start the journey with one step,
Give it all I've got with pep!
Knowing I'll be guided to the end.

In truth there really is no end;
Just a new place to begin.
Everything comes round again,
Everything comes round again.

THE VOICE:

Greg (Los Angeles, California)

Q: Why is the process of writing down and saying aloud what we wish to call forth so powerful?

It is because the first two levels of creation are enacted: thought and word. The action part is always derived from these crucial initial steps. There is also an energetic resonance when you use your own voice to speak these words. This process literally shifts the energy around you in profound ways, much like incantations were invoked in ancient times. This vibration reinforces and magnifies the energy of the underlying thought. Also, focusing on a particular desire for manifestation is more concentrated in its energy—more than an overall vision would have. The overall vision is your blueprint. The vocal, single askings—commands, if you will—are the highlights or additional supplemental desires that arise from your journey toward your overall vision.

Q: What is the best way to do it?

Write your desire by hand with a permanent marker or pen in large print on a nice clean piece of paper. This symbolizes permanence and clarity behind your intent. Display the message prominently at your work station. Then read it aloud as if you are addressing a room. You are announcing your intention, not apologetically whispering. Keep stating your message until it feels real and a part of your now. See it happening. Do this every day, and act on the inspiration that will come to you during this period until it manifests in physicality.

Q: How should I word it? "Dear God, I am so grateful that _____ is coming to me now?" or, "Dear God, thank You for creating _____ for me that I may experience this part of my grandest vision of who I am?"

Those are both good.

Chapter 2, Lesson #3

"Just Do It."

Remember that slogan for Nike athletic products from the '80s? Whoever the ad wizard was that came up with that one must have been especially proud because it was everywhere, nearly as omnipresent as God Itself! It was on billboards, bumper stickers, t-shirts, television commercials, bus ads, subway signs . . . just about everywhere you looked. The catchphrase "Just Do It" was so popular, in fact, that the First Lady of the United States at the time, Nancy Reagan, adopted it as a slogan promoting volunteerism. And a noble cause it was, inviting people who had never volunteered, to take that first step outside of their comfort zones, and just do it. If *Conversations with God* were to adopt a slogan meant to inspire people, it might be this:

"Just *Be* It."

Because as the concept in today's lesson states:

LIFE OPERATES ACCORDING TO THE BE-DO-HAVE PARADIGM.

CWG talks a lot about how most of us have it backward. We live our lives from a "have-do-be" place. We think we must *have* something before we can *do* something in order to *be* something. For example, if I have more time off, I can do what I want, then I'll be happy. Sound familiar?!

I think the reason we've got the "be-do-have" paradigm backward is because from our earliest years we were taught the value system of work/ reward. If we did this work, we could have that reward. Then once we had that reward, we could be happy, fulfilled, contented, or whatever it was we were wanting to be. In other words, "do-have-be."

In my growing-up years it looked like this: If my sisters and I did our chores, we could have our weekly allowance. If we baby-sat or helped Dad around the office, we could have a little more money, and could treat ourselves to lunch and shopping with our girlfriends on a Saturday. I remember my cousin Rob mowed lawns for several summers and saved enough money to buy his first car when he turned sixteen.

But what was really our reward for doing the work? Was the value inherently in the lunch or the shopping or the car? No. The money we girls spent on shopping and lunch with our friends helped us to have fun and feel happy, so the value was in being happy. The car that Rob bought with his hard-earned lawn-mowing money helped him to be free to come and go as he wished.

The reward was the state of being that those things we had worked for helped us achieve—happiness and freedom.

What *Conversations with God* wants us to understand about the "be-do-have" paradigm is this: We can decide to be anything we want, no matter what we have or what we're doing.

What if we kids had simply chosen to *be* happy and free, and then let what we did and what we had arise naturally from that place? In other words, "be-do-have" instead of "do-have-be" or "have-do-be"?

This is exactly what CWG invites us to do. Know why? Because when we think we must "do this" in order to "have that" before we can "be something," we postpone our joy. And when we feel we must "have this" in order to "do that" before we can "be something," again, we are putting our joy out there in the future somewhere. And since joy is our natural state of being, this goes against who and what we inherently are.

Why else does CWG invite us to decide who and what we want to be? Because that's the way God operates. God simply and powerfully states, "I am that, I am," and we can, too. When we are choosing to be something, and letting what we do and what we have flow naturally from that state of being, we are living the way God lives.

As we learned in our last lesson, we can choose this state of being in regard to our "calling," and declare for all to hear, "I am a _____."

We can also make a different kind of "beingness" statement—one that will help us move more smoothly through any situation life presents to us: We can decide ahead of time what aspect of the Divine we will be in any given moment.

Conversations with God, Book 1 says that God is always joyful, loving, accepting, blessing, and grateful. *Conversations with God, Book 3* further states that God is limitless, eternal, and free. Since we are each beloved individuations of the Divine, we share these characteristics. We can consciously choose to come from these, our natural states of being, and let all of our doing and having occur naturally as a result.

Talk about going with the flow!

⋄⋄⋄

Please write in your journal or post on the website your answers to the following Self-Reflection Questions:

1. What other aspects of God would you like to be? List as many as you can think of. Some examples might be: compassionate, generous, helpful, etc.

2. What do you think you might do differently than what you're doing now if you were to adopt each of these states of being?

3. What do you think you might have that you don't have now if you were to adopt each of these states of being?

The following are Action Steps for you to take over the next week:

1. When you wake up each morning, choose an aspect of Divinity that you will be for the day. Remind yourself frequently throughout the day what that aspect is, then continue to be it no matter what comes up that might normally pull you out of it. It might be helpful to put "sticky notes" in a few prominent places where you'll see them often. Please choose a different state of being every day and write about what experiences they bring you.

2. If you have a particularly challenging activity or event coming up, choose one or more states of being ahead of time that you think will help it go more smoothly for you and for the others involved. See how that works for you, then write about your experience.

◇◇◇

Postscript

Put the cart before the horse. Act as if. *Trust*, knowing that even before you ask, it is given.

Perhaps there is no subject that we in our modern society struggle with more than money. For a great number of us, it is a cause of constant concern. The perceived lack of money is often a low level stressor that is always in our subconscious and very often is what CWG calls the Sponsoring Thought behind our conscious thoughts, words, and actions. We are so used to living with this sense of lack that we often aren't even aware of it. Yet if we harbor worries about money, which are thoughts of non-abundance, it's hard to be completely happy, and we find ourselves dwelling in the "do-have-be" or the "have-do-be" mode of living.

So how can we, if we are carrying loads of debt or just living paycheck to paycheck, be completely happy in spite of that? Ah, yes, there's the rub. That is exactly the situation Greg and I found ourselves in, the last several years we lived in Nashville, and it was a constant challenge. Thank God those years coincided with our period of greatest spiritual growth. Looking back, I now see that our difficult financial situation was the catalyst for a lot of that growth. Please always remember the following aphorism, if you take away nothing else from this book:

OBSTACLES ARE OPPORTUNITIES.

All the challenges in our lives, even the biggest, most difficult life changes, are cross-roads that provide us with brand new opportunities to express the grandest version of our greatest vision of who we are. When we know this, the answer to the question, "Am I going to let this defeat me, or shall I rise above it?" is easy because we know inherently, when we ask it, which choice feels bad and which choice feels good. When we listen to our feelings we instantly know the answer.

We are invited by all of life's challenges, including financial ones, to be the highest and best we can be. I can't speak for you, but I've found that the only way I can be my best is by staying as closely aligned with God as possible—staying centered in the truth of who I really am, which is a part of that one Divine energy, endowed with all of Its aspects. When I remain focused on that, I can breathe into the difficulty and feel true peace. I can follow the advice in the famous song by Bobby McFerrin that says, "Don't worry. Be happy!"

When looking back at my CWGs through the years, I see that the single issue I asked for help with the most was money and how to stop worrying about it. To list here all of the supportive responses I received from *The Voice* could be a book in itself, but suffice to say, I was always told to be happy in spite of seemingly difficult financial circumstances, and to remember how wonderfully provided for I have always been. I was also advised to see money for the illusion it really is, so it could relax its grip on my mind. Even though it sometimes seems static, money is fluid. It flows in, and it flows out, and it serves us to try not to resist that; to be grateful in both the receiving *and* in the letting go of it. Perhaps most importantly, I was also advised to come from the *feeling* of being abundant, and to allow my thoughts, words, and actions to come from that feeling place.

So I did—the best I could, anyway. I soldiered on through the lean Nashville years, continuing to donate part of our meager income to charities and church, and "robbing from Peter to pay Paul" (borrowing from one credit card cash advance to pay off another), until a new opportunity finally presented itself. Now, here is where major trust came in. The time came to move to Los Angeles, and we were wisely advised to try it for a year first without selling the house. This path was pointed out to Greg and me by Neale himself, when Greg shared with him, "Santa Monica keeps coming up for me."

At first glance, this looked like a very expensive proposition—and it was! Keep paying all the bills on the Nashville house, find a new furnished place in LA to live, and pay for that, too? All the while, paying for a cat sitter and flights back and forth to be with them every month? Oh, and we would need a car in LA, too. Hmmm . . . Pretty expensive. More debt on top of debt. But guess what? The thought of it lit us both up so much, we knew something greater was brewing for us! Talk about going within to listen to *The Voice* a lot. That's the understatement of the year. In hindsight, there is no way I could have gotten from there to here with any peace at all had I not done my CWGs every step of the way, because I was extremely attached to our Nashville home and to living there. I remember leaving my sister Mary Margaret's pool party in tears one beautiful Saturday afternoon to fly back to LA. I told her, "This is the hardest thing I've ever done." I'm moved to tears right now, just recalling it. Thank God I told her, though, because the second I did, she dropped her frustration with me for, once again, following a dream and leaving her behind. Bless her heart. I love her so. It can't have been easy being my little sister all these years. "Don't fall in love with a dreamer," an old song says. I think I finally know what that song means.

What I really want to share with you here is this: Greg and I loved LA right away, so we both knew that this is where we were meant to be for the next segment of our lives. We felt very happy here, and because of that feeling of joy and the higher purpose behind it, the planets lined up to allow us to stay here. In the process, *the money problems took care of themselves.*

True enough, the debt got larger before this happened, but we were happy anyway. We "put the cart before the horse," moving to LA before getting the work. We chose to "act as if"—to come from a feeling of abundance, regardless of what our financial accounts looked like. We chose to *trust*, knowing that even before we asked for the means to make this move, they would be there. And lo and behold, they were. The very day after we paid a security deposit on a rental house we could move the cats into and call home, the money started pouring in. First, in the form of proceeds Greg received as stock for a movie score he had done several years prior. It had finally become valuable enough to liquidate, so we sold off just enough to get his much-delayed composer fee out of it. Then, six months later, our beloved Nashville house sold, right at the one year mark! This enabled us to pay off all the debt we'd been carrying, with plenty more to support us as we embarked on this new chapter in our lives.

We were even able to donate the sign for the Music City Center for Spiritual Living's new building in Nashville. Our church family had so beautifully supported us in our growth during those seven years, we wanted to commemorate our gratitude to them. Perhaps the greatest "keeper" from that church is their "Affirmation For Life" that I've shared excerpts from previously in this book. Here it is in its entirety:

Today I make this promise to myself:

I choose to live my life as a joyful experience.

I choose to keep my mind focused on love as the greatest power in my life.

I choose to create greater possibilities in my life than I ever imagined before.

I listen to the wisdom of *The Voice* within me, knowing it is

Divine Intelligence at work in my life. I trust it and I act on it.

I keep my mind and my heart open, ready to

accept joy and success, however they appear.

I celebrate these ideas as the truth in my life, now and always.

And so it is!

Notice please, the three sentences that say: "I choose . . . I choose . . . I choose . . ." The very first choice is to be joyful, and everything else flows from that. When we marry that state of being with listening to the wisdom of *The Voice* within us, the real power kicks in. At some point, I added the sentence, "I trust it and I act on it," because what good is it if we *listen* to the wisdom of *The Voice*, but don't *trust* it? Or if we *listen* to the wisdom of *The Voice* and *trust* it, but don't *act* on what we hear? It takes all three to get our lives to take off in the direction of our dreams.

It's a process, my friends—a never-ending process. For this reason, I find it helpful to offer the following prayer of Neale's whenever I find myself moving out of a positive state of being, whether it's due to money issues or anything else:

"Thank you, God, for helping me remember that this problem has already been solved for me."

THE VOICE

Annie (Nashville, Tennessee)

Q: Dear God, you know I am experiencing a lot of sadness from time to time around this move to LA. Please enlighten me on how I can more happily move forward. Thank you in advance for your insight into this. I want to feel happy about it.

Then feel happy about it. It's truly a choice, you know. Just choose to be happy, and let the "doingness" come from that place. When you start to feel sad about it, stop and change your mind. Pray to Me immediately for relief and with gratitude, knowing that this wouldn't be happening if it weren't perfect. Don't you want to play bigger? Don't you want to make a bigger difference in the world? Of course you do! That is why you are going to LA.

I have solved every possible dilemma for you already. Just tap in, and tap in frequently. Relax into the process, knowing that all is truly well. And don't worry. Be happy. It is a choice, plain and simple.

Every single time you get sad, come to this place within. You will leave feeling better, every single time. It's soul searching and marrying the mind and soul. Every person should know about this. Remember to share it with others so they don't mistakenly think that they need to seek answers outside of themselves.

Greg (Nashville, Tennessee)

To achieve something, do not try—be, instead. Surrender to the workings of the Universe. It is impossible for you to plan or figure out how to get to where you say you want to go. And only I know where that is anyway! Trust the process and don't push. If you are pushing on a door to open it, you are forcing things and are out of awareness of what is so. As you move toward a doorway, the door will open automatically for you.

Enter into every situation intending the best for everyone. If your intentions are genuine, they will want to work (play) with you. If you come from ego with trepidation and worry, hoping they will take you into their circle, your negative vibration will repel them. You don't need to prove yourself to anyone. Just be love and light—your work and talent are already obvious to them.

Center yourself each day in your evolving vision and take the actions you receive from this place of awareness. Expect your career to sky-rocket! But know that it will exceed your expectations if you surrender and don't push.

Chapter 2, Lesson #4

The last concept in this chapter is repeated over and over in the *Conversations with God* books, yet if you're like me, you may have not fully understood its message:

**THE PURPOSE OF LIFE IS TO RECREATE YOURSELF ANEW
IN THE NEXT GRANDEST VERSION OF THE GREATEST VISION
EVER YOU HELD ABOUT WHO YOU ARE.**

For years, whenever I read this, I always thought it was a "doingness" statement. What always came to mind for me was, "What is the highest and best thing I can do?" and I always applied it to my music career.

A little background here: When I graduated from college with a degree in music education I knew full well I had no intention of teaching music. I didn't know what I wanted to do for a living, but at my school there were only two options for music degrees in piano and voice: music performance or music education. To me a performance degree seemed useless, hence the major in education.

After graduating, though, I did start performing. I found I could make a good living playing piano and singing at restaurants, country clubs, and piano lounges. I was very fortunate that I could earn full-time pay for part-time work, and I loved it. I eventually started performing on cruise ships and in European piano bars, and I loved it even more. I figured I had it made, getting paid to sing and play piano, and getting to travel around the world for free.

When Greg and I married, we moved to Orlando, Florida, where I played and sang at a Walt Disney World resort for ten years. It was during this time that my sister Nancy shoved *Conversations with God, Book 3* under my nose and said, "Here, just pick one page and read it." She'd been trying to get me to read CWG since *Book 1* came out but I hadn't wanted to because at that point in my life, I was ambivalent as to whether God existed at all. I had lost my faith during my college years, so even knowing she is certifiably a genius, and these books had changed her life, I was resistant to reading them. Finally one night she just thrust it at me. Well, I'm eternally grateful to her because one page is all it took, and I was hooked!

So because today's concept about re-creating ourselves kept coming up again and again in my reading, I finally started listening when the tourists at Disney World asked me why I wasn't doing more with my music. First, their questions came in the form of, "Why aren't you recording CDs?" Then, "Why aren't you in Nashville?!" Knowing that God talks to us all the time, I eventually realized all these people were relaying messages from my Higher Self, letting me know there were bigger and better opportunities for me than just playing and singing in piano bars for the rest of my life.

And once I finally opened to the guidance I was receiving, I always followed it. This led to two country music CDs, a record deal in Nashville, three European tours, and most importantly, my relationship with Neale. The five weeks Greg and I spent traveling abroad with him, providing music for his lectures and workshops, gave us the perfect opportunity to assimilate the CWG messages more than ever. (If you've never had the pleasure of hearing Neale speak, I strongly encourage you to do so, either at one of his live events or online. What most people don't realize because he's so amazingly wise is, he's really funny!)

My passion for deeply integrating the messages of *Conversations with God* has led me to this writing, and I've continued to be guided every step of the way. I had no idea I would be teaching CWG until Neale announced it to the room at a retreat in Baltimore. After introducing me as one of the staff, he quietly stated, " . . .and Annie is working toward becoming a presenter of this material." Well, you could have knocked me over with a feather. That sure was news to me! Told ya he's wise.

So all of this *has* been a process of re-creating myself anew in the next grandest version of the greatest vision I ever held about who I am. It has also been a process of re-creating myself anew in the next grandest version of the greatest vision my Higher Self ever held about who I am because, as you can see, most of these changes certainly weren't ideas I had in mind!

What I have come to realize is this: The next grandest version of the greatest vision I have about myself now has little to do with choosing what I am doing. It has everything to do with choosing what I am *being*. I can sing and speak about CWG all day long, but if I step off the stage and act like a jerk to someone because I haven't consciously chosen to be kind, it negates every positive thing I just did. And believe me, there are plenty of famous singers who do just that.

We've looked at following our "calling" in this chapter, and we've also looked at choosing our states of being. I would argue that the latter is just as important as the former because no matter what we're doing, if we are being the very best we can be, that's what is going to make us feel happiest.

What does that look like? To me, it looks like being the most God-like, loving person I can be in every moment of every day. To love as God loves—that is the opportunity and the challenge.

Just for the record, I'm still working on this! I make bracelets based on one of my songs that say, "LOVE IS WHO I AM." CWG says we can substitute the word "love" for the word "God," and I had this in mind when I wrote the song.

These "Love Bracelets" serve to remind me, and all of us who wear them, to come from love in every situation. If I start to get irritated or upset or worried, I look at my bracelet and remember, "No, I am not those things. *Love* is who I am. *Love* is who I am."

And every time I remember to be love in every moment, I *am* re-creating myself anew in the next grandest version of the greatest vision ever I held about who I am.

<hr>

Please write in your journal or post on the website your answers to the following Self-Reflection Questions:

1. What is the next grandest version of the greatest vision ever you held about your "calling," or what you might choose to do for a vocation or avocation? Is it the same "calling" that you mentioned in Chapter 2, Lesson #2? Can you think of an even greater vision? If so, what would that look like for you?

2. What is the next grandest version of the greatest vision ever you held about your state of being?

The following are Action Steps for you to take over the next week:

1. In Chapter 2, Lesson #3, I asked you to list as many aspects of God that you could think of, and then asked you to adopt one each day. For the next week, please try to adopt *all* of them, all the time. To help you remember to do this, write down your list, and put it in several places where you'll see it often throughout each day.

2. Please write about any experiences this brings you.

◇◇

Postscript

Whenever I've pondered this lesson's concept, "The purpose of life is to re-create yourself anew in the next grandest version of the greatest vision ever you held about who you are," I've always done so with the future in mind. "What is my highest and best next step? What would I love to do now? Who do I choose to be now?"

It's interesting, also, to ponder this concept with the past in mind. Doing so illustrates that re-creation is the purpose of life. Ever since we were babies just learning to crawl, we set and reached new milestones for ourselves. Learning to walk, talk, and feed ourselves . . . Going to kindergarten and learning our ABCs and numbers . . . The excitement of beginning first grade! In my case, learning to write in cursive, taking piano lessons, auditioning for plays, trying out for cheerleader . . . On to middle school and high school with Spanish classes, concert choir, and many advanced subjects . . . Some of us went on to college, which held all new challenges of its own, not the least of which was learning to navigate through miles of red tape in order to graduate . . . All of these progressions through our growing up years show us that we are, and have always been, enlarging and expanding ourselves into grander versions of greater visions of who we might next become.

At some point in our adult years, though, many of us lose sight of our sense of purpose. After the initial excitement of starting out on our own, most of us eventually settle down into a job and home life, and sometimes the routine can cause us to become too comfortable or complacent. We might even feel compelled to stay in jobs we don't like, eventually allowing the daily grind to wear us down to the point where we lose hope for something better in life.

Ironically, some lose their sense of purpose for the exact opposite reason: They reach the pinnacle of success in their chosen field. Two iconic Americans come to mind, both of whom died very shortly after retiring. One is Charles Schulz, creator and animator of the world-famous "Peanuts" cartoons, who passed two months after announcing his retirement, the day before his last original comic strip was published. He had predicted that the strip would outlive him. The other is Bear Bryant, head football coach of the University of Alabama for twenty-five years. He took his teams to six national championships and thirteen conference titles, and when he retired in 1982, he held the record for most wins as a head coach in college football history. When asked after winning his final game what he would do after retirement, the great coach prophetically declared, "Probably croak in a week." He died of a massive heart attack four weeks later, the day after passing a routine medical checkup.

Both of these men had taken their careers to the ultimate level, and when each of them passed so soon after retirement, I remember thinking they must have felt they had no more purpose in life. Perhaps this was true, if their sense of self was tied to their outstanding careers.

Yet it doesn't have to be this way. My beloved Uncle Bob is a perfect example of someone who has consciously chosen to continue re-creating himself throughout his life. He was president of the student body at the University of Tennessee, and after graduating, eventually worked his way up to president and CEO of an advertising agency in Louisville, Kentucky. During his twenty-year tenure as president, he grew the business into the largest ad agency in the state. He served on a number of prestigious boards and worked on notable community development projects over the years. Also during this time, as busy as he was, he decided to start running 10k races and eventually marathons. He completed three of them, the last one being the New York Marathon in his 51st year.

Fast forward to retirement, and what did he do? Lie down and die? Oh, heck no! He must be the ultimate Renaissance man because he not only took up golf, he also dove fully into his latent talent of art, taking classes in sculpting and different kinds of painting. He now has a huge collection of beautiful watercolors and some of the most gorgeous rock sculptures I've ever seen. And even though he's had several surgeries including hip and shoulder replacements, that hasn't stopped him. He's still going strong, well into his 80s, and is one of the happiest men you'll ever meet. His former advertising agency gives the "Robert S. Allison Spirit Award" in his honor each year to an individual whose "enterprise, zeal, and enthusiasm most contributes to creating a positive culture and spirit" at the agency. Well done, Uncle Bob!

As you ponder this last lesson on Creation & Purpose, where do you find yourself at this point in your life? Are you still re-creating yourself anew in who you're choosing to be and what you're choosing to do about that? The fact that you're reading this book gives me a clue that you're probably quite interested in moving your life forward, or else you probably wouldn't still be reading it. If this is true, there's only one question to ask yourself:

Now what?!

THE VOICE

Greg (Los Angeles, California)

Q: I would like to know more about the creative process, particularly the method of calling forth an experience quickly—one that is a stepping stone to my larger vision.

This is a simple process, really. But it is not one that many people use commonly with a day-to-day frequency. Let's look at the process closely:

First, one must quiet the mind and be in a receptive mode, just as you are in now.

Then, make a summarizing statement of what you want to bring into your experience.

Think without forcing, and gently nudge your imagination along, allowing Spirit to guide you in your visualization. Since you have a limited perspective due to the nature of your physical existence, the power of the visioning process comes from outside yourself—your "imagineering" guide—for it is not possible for you to "see" the best experience.

When you do this, you are allowing yourself to be guided to the exact experience that will bring you and your soul the highest experience that you seek.

This atonement (at-one-ment) or alignment with the highest version of the experience you are calling forth will set forth a powerful vortex of the highest vibration and launch the visualized experience rapidly unfolded into your present. If you use this process to call forth a desire in you, the culmination, when it is experienced in your physical timeline, will be a completion of extraordinary satisfaction, joy, exuberance, and growth. Instead of, "Okay, now what?" after the completion, you will feel more like, "Wow! What's next?!"

And so by aligning more accurately with your soul's desire, the manifestation will be more joyful. This process will also allow you and your soul to call forth many more experiences that declare who you are in this physical-ity. You/you will be playing on the same team with the same agenda. You will feel continually energized, and opportunities will continuously be flooding into your experience.

You will find that the feelings you have when visualizing the desired experience will be powerful and therefore exponentially impactful, resulting in an almost immediate manifestation. This is what joyful living is all about.

Chapter 3

DISPELLING A FEW MISCONCEPTIONS

Chapter 3, Lesson #1

Welcome to the first lesson in Chapter 3. In the next four weeks we will look deeply at several concepts from *Conversations with God* that will aid us as we work together toward "Dispelling A Few Misconceptions."

Before we came into these wonderful human bodies here on Earth, we existed happily with God, our Source, in the Spiritual Realm of the Absolute, and we knew exactly who we were: inseparable parts of God, who is Omniscient (All-Knowing), Omnipotent (All-Powerful), and Omnipresent (All Things Everywhere). We knew, quite logically, that it is impossible to be separate from All Things Everywhere, and we knew intuitively that we, too, were All-Knowing and All-Powerful. Pretty wonderful, huh?!

As soon as we came into our bodies as babies in the Physical Realm of Relativity, however, we began to pick up flawed premises which limit our freedom here. And when we don't feel totally free, it's difficult to feel totally happy. We will learn over the next four weeks that these limitations are self-imposed and are based on false beliefs. Then we can begin to see what's really true, and set ourselves free.

Let's start with what may be one of the most controversial concepts that *Conversations with God* invites us to remember:

THERE'S NO SUCH THING AS RIGHT AND WRONG.

That's a doozy! If I said that to my mother right now, she would look at me as if I were crazy, and probably lament that she did a terrible job raising me. I swear, if I had a dollar for every time my mom said, "Go to your room and think about what you did wrong," I could eat out for a week! Sometimes I wished she'd just spank me and get the punishment over with because she'd make me stay in my bedroom for what seemed like hours. There was no TV or phone in my room, and I wasn't allowed to read, so I had lots of time to deeply consider the trouble I'd gotten into and why. In hindsight, of course, this was the perfect "punishment," because it set me up for a lifetime of thinking about what seemed right and what seemed wrong.

What I always came away from those experiences with was an ability to look at two sides of any story. I think that's why I was the "peacemaker" between two battling sisters and why people have always come to me for help with their problems. You can't give effective advice if you only see one person's point of view. You must be able to see from different perspectives and observe impartially what someone did that worked for them and what they did that didn't work for them. In order to do this, you must know what their objectives were to begin with.

CWG says there is no such thing as *absolute* right and wrong. Rather, there is only what works and what doesn't work, given what it is you are trying to do or where it is you are wanting to go. If you are trying to be a policeman, it doesn't work to go to nursing school. It isn't wrong. It just doesn't get you where you're wanting to go.

Now, most people would say that murdering another human being is absolutely wrong, or the rape of an innocent woman or child is absolutely wrong. And for most of us, these are acts that we cannot imagine ourselves doing because they would be totally out of alignment with who we've decided we are. So for us, these actions feel very wrong. But in order to believe that these actions are *intrinsically* wrong, one would have to believe that something can happen that is outside of God's will. And since God is Omniscient, Omnipresent and Omnipotent, this is impossible.

CWG also tells us that no one does anything inappropriate given their model of the world. The person who does something that almost all of us see as being terribly wrong either has it in his mental construction that what he's doing is okay, or if he feels it's not okay, he does it anyway because he believes it is in his best interest.

But what about those times when *we* feel deep down that we've done something wrong? Not because society says so, but because we feel so bad we can't stop feeling guilty about it?

We are each blessed with the most wonderful guidance system within us—our *feelings*. We know what feels right and what feels wrong to us at a gut level. When we feel terrible about something we've done, it isn't because what we did was inherently wrong. It's because what we did was out of alignment with who we've decided we are.

According to CWG, guilt and fear are the only enemies of mankind, and these feelings, if allowed to continue unexamined and unabated, can cause not only great emotional stress, but also an eventual wearing down of the body. So if we have a guilty conscience about something, it's always good to figure out why we feel that way. Often, we will find we didn't act in harmony with our highest knowing, and the reliving of this action in our mind is keeping us out of alignment with our soul.

It would benefit us to make amends not only with the other person or persons involved, but also with ourselves. The statement from *Conversations with God* that says, "No one does anything inappropriate given their model of the world," isn't just for other people. We must offer *ourselves* compassion, understanding, and forgiveness before we can move on, into the joyous existence for which we came.

Please write in your journal or post on the website your answers to the following Self-Reflection Questions:

1. Do you think it's possible to feel guilty for something you did simply because society says it's wrong? Looking back at the times in your life when you've had a guilty conscience about something, was it because society said what you did was wrong, or because you felt in your heart and soul that it was wrong for you? Please explain the circumstances.

2. Name at least three things that society said were wrong that have changed in your lifetime—things that society now says are okay. It doesn't have to be the society where you live; it may be that of another culture or country.

3. If you believe, as CWG says, that nothing can happen to the soul against its will, do you think anyone can do something absolutely wrong to another? If so, what would it be?

4. Can you think of anything that seems absolutely wrong to you? If so, please try to prove your point.

5. If you gave up the need to be right about anything and everything, what would you do differently?

The following are Action Steps for you to take over the next week:

1. Look into your past to see if anyone did something to you that still feels unforgivable. Work very hard to try to see what happened from their point of view, and if it aligns with your soul to do so, reach out to that person to make amends. Please write in your journal or post on the website about this process.

2. Look into your past to see if you ever did anything for which you haven't forgiven yourself. Work very hard to offer yourself compassion, under-standing, and forgiveness. Please write about how this is working for you.

3. Look into the history of the world for anyone and everyone who did something to someone else that still seems unforgivable to you. Work very hard to try to see what happened from all perspectives. Realize that there may be something you don't understand about the situation, the under-standing of which could change your mind about it. Please write out your thought process about this.

Postscript

When trying to help people move through the pain of unresolved past trauma, sometimes the biggest hurdle is helping them understand what happened from their soul's point of view, especially if the person has been carrying around negativity about a perceived "wrong" for many years. It can be even more difficult to help people who have such a genius mind they exist almost purely in it, without ever looking at the events of their lives from the perspective of their soul. Many times these people are so certain that what happened *shouldn't* have happened, this line of thinking remains at the forefront of their minds for a very long time, resulting in poor health and even premature old age. This, of course, is only natural because how can a body thrive when its caretaker constantly subjects it to negative thinking, judgment, and blame? Eventually the mental consternation wears it down. The dis-ease of the mind manifests as disease of the body.

Sometimes it's only after all other avenues of conventional treatment have been exhausted that people look for spiritual solutions to relieve them of their mental anguish. One technique I've learned from Neale to try to help these people is the SouLogic process. You can read his explanation of it and watch a video demonstration here:

http://www.nealedonaldwalsch.com/doc/soulogicprocess

SouLogic is a series of seven questions designed to help people re-contextualize painful events or relationships from their past in order to achieve peace and clarity around them. The questions are these:

1. Do you believe in God?

2. Do you believe in the existence of the human Soul?

3. What do you believe is the relationship between the Soul and God?

4. Can anything happen to God that God does not want to have happen?

5. Can anything happen to your Soul that your Soul does not want to have happen?

6. Why would your Soul seek to bring you the experience that is now being discussed?

7. If there is another person involved in this experience, why do you think the Soul of that other person would join you in co-creating this experience?

When a person does this process with a genuinely open mind, the old story of "I was right" and "you were wrong" is almost always dropped in a new, clear, "aha" moment.

I like the analogy of looking at life as a tapestry. To most of us, the Physical Realm is rather like the back side of the tapestry. All the different colored threads are jumbled together in what looks like a chaotic, tangled mess that makes no sense. Each of us are as one of those tiny threads in the midst of countless others, seemingly encompassed in a state of disarray.

When we turn the tapestry over to the front side, however, we see the way all the threads come together to form a breathtakingly beautiful, perfect design. I think it will be sort of like this when we cross over to the Spiritual Realm, because we'll be able to see the big picture from "the other side."

The challenge, of course, is to try to see the perfection while we're still here living life, instead of waiting until our transition day. The best way I know how is to stop making everyone wrong and to trust that all is well and good in God's world. As CWG notes in a light-hearted little joke, God hasn't made a mistake in a very long time!

THE VOICE

My dear friend and co-songwriter Gregory Fisher has, thankfully, resumed his email blogs that I find ever inspiring! As we know, *The Voice* can speak to us in an infinite number of ways. For this lesson's quote, I will let you read it in the form of Gregory's insightful blog dated June 17, 2016. You can sign up to receive his free emails here: *https://gregoryfisher.life*

Gregory (Nashville, Tennessee)

My brother died two weeks ago. He was only 65. He died very suddenly and unexpectedly. It has been awful.

Partly it was awful because we had unfinished business. Over the past few decades, our relationship became strained when he and his wife learned that I was gay. We had moments where it seemed we were going to get past our differences and disappointments. Ultimately, we had barely spoken in the past five years.

In addition to that, my brother and my mother had also experienced some conflict through the last five years of her life. I, of course, blamed him. Nothing is ever that simple.

All of that to bring you to what happened next.

On the night after he died, I had a very vivid dream. Now, let me explain that I virtually never dream. I experience sleep apnea, so most nights I don't get deeply enough into REM sleep to dream. But I had a dream that night.

In the dream, I walked into a room that seemed like a place in the afterlife. Seated comfortably there were my mother and my brother. They were holding hands and smiling up at me. Everything was very loving and tranquil.

As I approached them, my mother began to speak:

You see, there are only two ways to communicate with another person. One is from a place of needing to be right, and the other is from a place of needing to be love.

Then she delivered the punch line:

And you can't communicate from both at the same time.

That was it. I woke up and knew that everything was alright. There was no unfinished business between them or me.

You see, beloved one, once our egos are gone, and in that place, there is no need to be right, only a need to be love.

All I can say now is, "On Earth as it is in heaven."

Chapter 3, Lesson #2

What is God's will? I invite you to step away from this text and close your eyes for five minutes and really ponder this question:

WHAT IS GOD'S WILL?

See you back here in five.

I've been thinking about this question for the past week, knowing that in today's lesson I would try to convey my truth about the following concept:

GOD WANTS NOTHING AND REQUIRES NOTHING.

That's another doozy. Have you ever thought about how the vast majority of people believe that God *does* have an agenda in our lives, and it's our job to follow it . . . or else?! The problem with this belief is that an unspoken, impossible task is implied. How can we possibly *follow* God's agenda in our lives if we don't know what it is? Ah, no problem, say the great faiths of the world. Our book will tell you exactly what you're supposed to do.

Depending on where in the world you were born, and to whom, you were likely brought up with the writings of a particular book that your society decided was the correct book to follow in order to do God's will. Being raised in the southern United States, our society's book was most definitely the Bible. And although my mother and sisters and I were members of a small Episcopal church which focused more on ritual, using *The Book of Common Prayer*, people in the rest of our community, including my father, were often seen carrying their Bibles around and quoting from them. It was a foregone conclusion that the Bible contained everything we needed to know about what God wanted and what God required of us.

But what about the books in the rest of the world? As we grew up and learned there was a much bigger world out there, and people in other places relied on *other* books to tell them what they were supposed to do, the logical question had to follow in the thinking person's mind: Which book is correct? What if our book isn't the end-all that Dad says it is? And if the Bible doesn't necessarily have it right, then what *does* God really want and require of us?

Let's look up the word "want" in *Webster's American Dictionary*. The transitive verb "want" has the following definitions:

1. to lack

2. to crave (he wants love)

3. to desire (he wants to travel)

4. to wish to see or apprehend (wanted by the police)

5. [chiefly British] to require

It's interesting that in British English, the words "want" and "require" mean the same thing. In American English, a requirement is not a wanting. To require something is to imply that one must have it. To want something is to wish for it. Webster's American definition of "require" is:

1. to insist upon; demand; order

2. to need

Let's plug these definitions into our concept, shall we?

• God lacks nothing.

• God craves nothing.

- God desires nothing.

- God wishes to see nothing.

- God insists upon, demands, and orders nothing.

- God needs nothing.

Now that we have a frame of reference, we can get into the meat of our discussion. So let's take these ideas point by point and see how we feel about them, using logic and common sense.

God lacks nothing. This feels very true to me. How can God, who is Omnipresent—the source and substance of All Things Everywhere—lack anything? It's impossible.

God craves nothing. Again using Webster's definition, to crave is "to ask for earnestly; beg," and "to long for eagerly." Well, we certainly know that God doesn't need to ask for anything "earnestly." To do so implies pleading. Who would God plead *to*? Does God beg? Of course not. And does God "long for" anything "eagerly"? I don't think so because that would imply that there is a gap of time between what God would "long for" and the time it would take for God to manifest it. According to CWG and many physicists (Einstein included), the passage of time is an illusion, so again, this is impossible.

God desires nothing. Now, this is one we're all going to have to come to our own conclusions about. I believe God *does* have one basic desire, and that is to know Itself in Its own experience. That is, CWG explains, why God created the Realm of the Physical. If God had been content to know Itself without experiencing what It knew, God would have remained forever only where It already was, in the Realm of the Absolute. But CWG says God wanted to experience what It knew Itself conceptually to be, so It created our illusory Physical Realm for that purpose.

One may also say that God desires to expand Itself, but this is really part of the one basic desire, to know Itself in Its experience. We are adding to God's expansion by adding to our own, here in the Physical Realm, but according to *Book 2*, the time will come when all physicality will contract again into a single point that is inconceivably compact, smaller than the head of a pin. Then another big bang will occur, life will again expand, then contract, then expand again, then contract again . . . on and on it goes. This is breathtakingly (!) the breathing in and out of God. So yes, I believe that God desires to do this, or it would not be so.

God wishes to see nothing. God already sees everything, so I'm cool with this one.

God insists upon, demands, and orders nothing. This, for me, is obvious, although I know that many people would probably not agree. But envision with me, if you will, what kind of God this would be. I see a judge pounding his fist on his bench, stating loudly what must be done. I just don't buy into this at all. A God who insists upon things, makes demands, and orders people around, just sounds to me like a very non-powerful God who is trying to make himself feel more powerful by asserting what little power he has, kind of like a bully! Most religions agree that God is Omnipotent. One who possesses all the power in the world has no need to make demands of others because It has the power to do anything It wants Itself.

God needs nothing. Again, because God is All Things Everywhere, for God to need anything would defy logic. It's impossible to need what you are.

Now, there's one other point I want to address. The logical argument can be made that God *does* have wants and requirements because *we* do, and we are part of God. In the Realm of the Absolute this is not the case, but here in the Realm of the Physical, we've forgotten that we have the same power to create instantaneously that God has. Interestingly, this brings us full circle, back to that book we were talking about earlier. The Bible would not exist in its current form were it not for one particularly exceptional man, Jesus of Nazareth, who came to Earth to remind us who we really are and who demonstrated it in his life and death, and even beyond.

The Bible says—correctly, I believe—that God made mankind in Its image, but when we project our human wants and needs onto God, we incorrectly make It into *our* image, and believe this ill-conceived God to be the truth of who and what It is. But just because we believe it does not make it so.

So what *is* God's will? God only desires *what It already is*. And because God is all there is, if It were to have requirements, they would only be of Itself. This would be illogical, don't you think?

<hr />

Please write in your journal or post on the website your answers to the following Self-Reflection Questions:

    1. Is there anything in your life you're doing right now that you don't really *want* to do but think you're *supposed* to do? If so, why are you doing it? Is

it because you think someone else wants you to? If so, who, and what do you think would happen if you stopped doing it?

2. If you could truly believe that God doesn't care one iota what you do or don't do, would your life be any different? How? Please explain.

3. If you have children, do you place requirements on them? What if, instead of requirements, you were to give them choices, tell them what the consequences would be, then let them make their own decisions? Do you think that would work for you and the child?

The following are Action Steps for you to take over the next week:

1. If you are involved in any relationships where you and/or the other person are putting requirements on each other, if it feels right for you, seek to amend the relationship to be one of total allowing. Remember, one aspect of God that we share is freedom. The happiest of relationships are those in which each person allows the other to be totally free. If you try this, please write in your journal or post on the website about your experience.

2. Make a list of the things you currently want most in your life, then look to see, one by one, what would happen if they never manifest. Would life go on for you pretty much the way it is now? Will you still be okay in five years if you don't get them? What's the worst that can happen if you don't get these things you want? Now, close your eyes and use your imagination to help you feel how it would be to *have* these things, one at a time. Know deeply that in

God's world where there is no such thing as want or lack, each one of these things already exists for you. Practice staying in a state of joyous openness to all good things so that each one may manifest in your experience. But do not put specific requirements on God's fulfillment of them for you. Your prayer might be as follows: "Thank you, God, for this or something better."

3. Read *What God Wants*. If you've read it before, please read it again.

⋄⋄⋄

Postscript

Do you place wants and requirements on life? *Conversations with God* says we can use the words "life" and "God" interchangeably, so, put another way, do you place wants and requirements on God? If so, and you don't get them, how does this affect your faith?

It's one thing to play around with the Law of Attraction, not getting the results you want, and conclude, "This stuff doesn't work." There are understandable reasons people sometimes come to that conclusion, but it isn't because the law doesn't work. It's because their understanding of how it works is incomplete and/or because they are not a clear vibrational match to what they want. Often, their Sponsoring Thought is overriding their conscious thought, so the majority of their focus is on the very thing they *don't* want—which, of course, draws it into their experience.

It's another thing entirely to not get what you want in life and to blame God for it. Or to take an even harder line, to look at one's difficult past or at the craziness of the world and conclude that there *is* no God. This is also understandable because the thinking mind wants to know, "What kind of God would allow *this* to happen?!" Yet is it wise to "throw the baby out with the bathwater"? To decide, based on an incomplete understanding of how life works, that there *is* no God? This is placing quite a requirement on God, don't you think? "If you don't show up the way I want you to, I'm just not going to believe in you. So there!"

Perhaps we could find it easier to accept things as they are if we understood more clearly how life is set up for us here in the Realm of the Physical, also aptly called the Realm of Illusion.

When we're born, we are given a clean slate on which to draw our next experience. Since God has given us free will with no strings attached (although some religious teachings would have us believe otherwise), we are free to think, say, do, and be anything we choose. The overriding reason we are here is for the evolution of the soul, and there are an infinite number of ways we can play this game of life in order to achieve that. Yet, as lovely as the idea might seem, not one of us would be served by living in Utopia. If there were no difficulties to challenge us, growth and expansion would be stymied. It is the conflict and what we choose to do about it that gives us the opportunity to shape and hone who we are. This is the ultimate response-ability.

With each passing day, I see more and more evidence that everything happening here has a spiritual reason behind it. Contracts with friendly souls are made before we cross into this illusory playground, knowing with full certainty where we will return after we're complete with the game. Knowing without a shadow of a doubt that we'll be totally cared for and supported while we're here. And knowing that as soon as we're finished here, all our souls need to do is shift their focus back into the Realm of the Absolute and the Realm of Illusion falls away.

My friend Sandy says life is like a "holodeck" on *Star Trek*. We create the virtual reality program, the "holodeck" runs it, we enter into it happily and expectantly ready to play, and whenever we're complete with the game, we simply say, "Computer, end program," and the virtual reality disappears.

If it's true that we are made in God's image and God doesn't require anything from us, I think the least we can do is reciprocate! If I want to live and love as God does—and I do—then the onus is on me to drop all of my requirements, including those I place on life to deliver those things I imagine myself to want. Of course, it's wonderful to have desires because they are the catalyst for the growth we came here for. Without them, we would never be inspired to do anything, and nothing would ever get done. The fine line we are invited to walk, however, is to not *require* them for our inner peace and joy. To choose to be happy no matter what happened in our yesterdays, no matter what is happening today, and no matter what may happen in our tomorrows. To be in a place of total allowing of what is, no matter how "bad" it may seem. To drop all requirements of anything to look a certain way. This is the pathway to peace.

THE VOICE

The next contributor's CWG is one of a few I included in this book that came through in the first person, from her own point of view. Please be aware that this may be the way *The Voice* speaks to you as well.

Colleen (Nashville, Tennessee)

I was struggling with a deep want for understanding and clarity with things that had happened. I kept thinking that those things would cause me to finally be able to release the hurt. If I could just get my daughter to explain everything . . . I instantly heard a *Voice*:

> *NOTHING anyone else does, or has ever done, is about me. None of my "betrayals" were anything other than my imagination. No one betrayed me; there is nothing to forgive. They were only there at my calling.*

I understood that "they" did not only include my daughter and the boys, it included everyone involved, even myself. I had contracted for the experience and they were my friendly souls.

Chapter 3, Lesson #3

The third concept in our "Dispelling A Few Misconceptions" chapter is a premise that is built on the last two concepts we've just explored: "There is no such thing as right and wrong," and "God wants nothing and requires nothing." One would have to believe at least one of those concepts in order to believe this one:

**THERE IS NO SUCH PLACE AS HELL,
AND ETERNAL DAMNATION DOES NOT EXIST.**

I mentioned in our last lesson that my dad is a big believer in the Bible. He considers it to be an infallible document and the only source of God's word, and the older he gets, the more he seems concerned about whether I believe it too. He actually told me a few years ago that he fears for my soul. But in order for me to believe everything he believes, I think I would've had to have been indoctrinated in it much earlier in life. Thankfully, my sisters and I were given the freedom to choose our church when we were very young.

Dad was a member of the rural southern Baptist church he was raised in, and Mom was a member of the small Episcopal church in our little town. My earliest memories are of going to church with Dad on one Sunday, then to Mom's church the next, then back to Dad's, then back to Mom's . . . Let me illustrate what that was like because the experiences could not have been more different.

The memory of the pastor at my dad's country Baptist church is forever ingrained in my mind because, to me, he looked sort of like Elvis Presley! He wore pastel-colored polyester leisure suits and had thick dark hair that he wore combed back in a very high pompadour. What I remember most, though, is being scared to death of him. He was all fire and brimstone, and he yelled bombastically at his congregation from the pulpit. I guess he figured his job was to frighten the beJesus out of everybody to make sure his flock was spared from hellfire and damnation. So as much as my sisters and I loved Dad, we didn't really like going to his church. Remember, feelings are the language of the soul, so our uncomfortable feelings were an indication that this was perhaps not the most positive place for us to be. Even the music didn't resonate with me.

Now imagine, if you will, what we girls experienced on those alternating Sundays at Mom's Episcopal church: beautiful stained-glass windows, gorgeous Gregorian chants and Bach chorales with pipe organ accompaniment, and the fascinating ritual of Holy Communion. Although we were too young to partake of the communion, we still received a sweet hands-on blessing by the priest at the altar rail every Sunday. And most important of all was the love in that church. It brings tears to my eyes as I remember it because the love I felt from God and the people there helped me endure the terror of corporal punishment I received regularly at home from my mom. The serenity I found in that tiny chapel helped me remain fundamentally happy in the knowledge and love of God.

So it didn't take long before we girls just naturally turned away from what we perceived as the church of fear, and embraced the church of love. I was fascinated to find later in life that *Conversations with God* says there are two basic emotions, fear and love! I'm sure I'm over-simplifying the modus operandi of Dad's Baptist church, but that's how my childhood mind saw it. In hindsight, it's astonishing to me how the congregation just sat there, willfully accepting that fear-based teaching, because it is so out of alignment with the truth of who we really are, which is love.

I'll never forget coming home from an Episcopal catechism class one day and telling my dad about it. I think I was eleven years old at the time. Dad asked me if they were teaching us about hell, and I said no, because the Episcopal church didn't really focus on that. He then told me outright that my Jewish friends who I carpooled to school with every day were going to hell when they die because "they don't accept Jesus Christ as their lord and savior." This really concerned me, so the next Sunday I asked Father Bill if what my dad had said was true. He gave me the most unexpected reply:

"What do *you* think?"

Wow, I thought. You mean I get to decide this for myself?! I told him, "No, I don't think they're going to hell because they're nice people." To my logical eleven-year-old mind, that was the only thing that made sense. I was beginning to see how large the world is, and I knew there were many millions of people who hadn't had a chance to hear about Jesus yet. I knew it would be extremely unfair for those people to be damned for what they didn't know, through no fault of their own. I also knew it just didn't make sense for Jewish people to be damned to hell simply because they don't believe the same things about Jesus that Christians do.

I came to find out later in life that it's not only Christians who believe in a fiery place called hell. According to Wikipedia, Gehenna is mentioned in the Hebrew Bible as a place where apostate (non-believing) Israelites and followers of other Gods "sacrificed their children by fire," and in Rabbinical Jewish, Gahenna "was a destination of the wicked." In the Qur'an, Jahannam is "a place of torment for sinners or the Islamic equivalent of Hell."

According to *The Encyclopedia of Hell,* Hindus have a hell of their own, but fortunately for them, since they believe in reincarnation, it is only temporary—"merely a stopping point where souls burn off evil before proceeding to the next life." Likewise, the Buddhist tradition includes "many temporary Hells where bad KARMA is burned away."

CWG says there is no such thing as karma in the traditional sense. We are much more powerful than that! It's plain to see, though, that people all over the globe have a lot of work to do if we truly wish to free ourselves from such false limiting beliefs. My friend Gregory wisely says, "Sometimes letting go of the lie we have innocently accepted is a tough job."

Thanks to the bravery and popularity of many New Thought speakers and authors, Neale Donald Walsch being preeminent to most of us here, large numbers of people are now coming to realize that they have misconstrued this idea of hell and are letting go of their fear of God. And those of us who felt this way intuitively as children are receiving corroboration of our beliefs. Even Pope John Paul II said in 1999 that we've had a mistaken notion of what hell really is. Neale quotes him in *Home with God: In a Life That Never Ends*: "Rather than a place, hell indicates the state of those who freely and definitively separate themselves from God, the source of all life and joy."

In CWG, God told Neale, "My will for you is your will for you." Most Christians believe that God has given us free will, but it comes with a stipulation: We must freely choose to accept Jesus Christ as our savior, or we'll be damned to hell. What kind of free will is that?!

The reason God has given us free will is because God's essence is freedom. Since we are part of God, we share the same aspects. We are free to think, say, and do anything we "damned well please" and not be damned for it! Now, if we choose to "freely and definitively separate ourselves from God, the source of all life and joy," we may, indeed, experience a self-induced mental version of hell. But the good news is, we have the power to change our minds and release ourselves from it. I know. I've gone through this process more than once. And although I didn't "freely and definitively" separate myself from God on purpose—I created it by default and misunderstanding—it felt like hell just the same. The road to recovery took a couple of years the first two times I experienced depression, but the last time, thanks to CWG, I got over it much more quickly.

In God's world, heaven is all there is, thank goodness, and we will realize it sooner or later. If not during our physical lifetime, then we'll remember when we cross back into the Realm of the Absolute.

I think it will be fun to be re-united there with Dad, where we can both look at life as it really is. I hope we'll share a chuckle or two at how caught up we got in the game!

Please write in your journal or post on the website your answers to the following Self-Reflection Questions:

1. Why do you suppose the major religions of the world all have their own version of hell?

2. Do you think people can be trusted to do their highest and best if they don't fear hell and damnation?

3. If you thought you could do anything in the world you wanted to and still go to heaven, would you do anything differently? Please elaborate.

4. If you wanted to teach people that the religions of the world have mistaken notions of hell, how would you explain it to them? How about to your kids?

The following are Action Steps for you to take over the next week:

1. Look for a spiritual community in your area that shares your beliefs in a loving God who embraces all and damns nothing (if that *is* how you believe!). It might be a Unity Church, a Center For Spiritual Living, or someone informally hosting a *Conversations with God* or *A Course In Miracles* study group. Attend one of their meetings and see how it feels for you to be around other people of like mind. If you like it, go again! If the first group you meet doesn't resonate with you, see if there's another one you can try.

2. Consider starting your own *Conversations with God* spiritual study group if there isn't one in your area. Neale has made it extraordinarily easy with his *Conversations with God Companion* guidebook. It has everything you need to dive right into the material in a way that makes the CWG concepts very functional in your life.

If you're interested in finding or creating a CWG study group, please visit the Conversations with God Foundation's study groups page on its website: *cwg.org*

As Neale said, "The fastest way to learn something is to teach it. Do not wait, therefore, until you 'know all about it' or have 'mastered' what you wish to share before you begin to share it. The world needs more of what you wish to *learn* more of."

Postscript

All hell is self-created. Friends, the mind is such a powerful thing—way more powerful than most of us realize. Unless we have some sort of mental illness (which can be a hell of its own), how we choose to think creates how we experience the events in our lives. We can free ourselves to live in heaven on Earth or damn ourselves to live in the hell of our own minds.

While pondering this idea in the wee hours of the morning, I got to wondering, what is the overriding way people create hell for themselves? What does the 50-year old woman who continually dwells on thoughts of her childhood abuse have in common with the 25-year old man who decides to arm himself to the teeth, walk into a gay bar, and kill fifty people? For that matter, what do they have in common with Adolph Hitler, who arguably instigated the most hellish scenario on Earth in recent memory? While perusing this, one thing came to mind:

NON-ACCEPTANCE.

The woman who absolutely will not drop the idea that someone in her past did her wrong—her refusal to accept what happened—creates her own private hell. The man who looks around him at people whose lifestyle he condemns and then murders them for it—his refusal to accept what's happening—creates his own public hell. The dictator who was steadfast in his belief that his race was the superior one *oozed* non-acceptance. And as we've seen with the escalation of random terrorist attacks, just as we saw in World War II, these men were so miserable in their own minds, they chose to create scenarios that made others miserable, too, resulting in untold sorrow.

What I've noticed about non-accepters is, they go from person to person, from book to book, from video to video, from website to website, trying to find others willing to affirm that they are right. They are so steadfast in their certainty that their point of view is correct, they will search high and low to prove it to themselves—and they usually find corroboration somewhere, from someone. It's when two or more people who share these extreme points of view of non-acceptance are gathered together that they become dangerous. It's almost as if they follow the, "If I fall, you're going down with me," line of thinking.

Now, just to be clear, it's taken me a lot of soul-searching over many years to get to a place of acceptance of "what is," and I'm still not there 100% of the time. The catalyst for the progress I've made, though, has surely been *Conversations with God*. Remember, the Five Attitudes of God are joyful, loving, *accepting*, blessing, and grateful. As an individuation of the Divine, these are my natural states of being, too. To live from them is to see the world the way It does, with no judgment. The challenge is to accept *everything*, knowing it's for the highest and best, or it wouldn't be happening.

I think the last thing I had to work hard to get over was our male cat, Gilligan's, sometimes excessive hunting behavior. He's such an effective hunter, one day he killed and ate not just one bird, but *three*. Aargh! I *love* our songbirds.

Of course, it's perfectly natural in the animal kingdom for carnivores to hunt, chase, and kill, but it's always been a matter of consternation for me. While watching nature documentaries, I've always rooted for the antelope to get away, and I still have to turn my head before the lion catches its prey. Truthfully, I really can't watch shows like that anymore. I'm too much of an animal lover, and that's why I've eaten no animals except fish for over 25 years. I hardly even eat fish anymore because I love them, too!

Anyway, Gilligan is the most effective hunter cat I've ever known, so much so that our nickname for him is "Kill-again"! He loves to bring his "catch of the day" into the house, announcing it loudly as he comes through the cat door. I used to get quite upset and scold him for it, but over time, I've come to accept it—most of the time. Some days I even tell him he's a good boy, then try not to look too closely as I clean up the mess! My non-acceptance of his behavior surely doesn't serve him or me, and when I'm able to relax about it, it loses its charge.

Is there anything that happened in your past that you still don't accept? Is there anything happening now that you don't accept? Please note, I didn't say, "that you don't agree with." Acceptance and agreement are two different things. I certainly don't agree with terrorist attacks and war, but I do accept them. Why? Two reasons: First, I really do believe that God makes no mistakes. Everything that happens is for evolution, which means it's for the highest good overall. What I used to think were "bad things happening to good people," I now think are soul pacts and contracts. I've heard about too many instances of this to believe otherwise. Second, it makes no sense to argue with life because it ends up hurting me the most. The two times in my life that I took my non-acceptance to the extreme, I ended up depressed for a couple of years both times. What I later realized was, it wasn't the circumstances themselves that were making me miserable. It was just my thoughts about them, and they were simply thoughts of . . . let's say it again:

NON-ACCEPTANCE.

It was only when I let go of not accepting what was happening and started looking for some glimmer of good in them that I was able to escape the hell of my own mind.

THE VOICE

Annie (Nashville, Tennessee)

You are the creator of your own reality because you are the thinker of the thought in your now moment.

Faith does not ask us to turn a blind eye, nor does it ask us to bury our head in the sand. Faith invites us to look at the big picture—to see the forest even when we're in the midst of the trees. Faith invites us to open up our vision and trust. Faith is having hindsight in the present moment.

Chapter 3, Lesson #4

I've realized as I've written these lessons for our chapter on misconceptions that I sure questioned a lot when I was growing up, and I often came to my own logical conclusions. This is especially true about today's concept:

DEATH DOES NOT EXIST.

One of my earliest memories of elementary school is a number line that was taped to the wall just above the chalkboard in the front of the classroom. This was a very long chart with a horizontal line that ran the entire length of the wall. In the middle of the line was a dot with its corresponding number "0." All the numbered dots on the right side of "0" were the positive numbers, "1" — "100," and after "100" the line became an arrow pointing to the right. This was to signify infinity; these positive numbers went on forever and never stopped. Likewise, on the left side of "0" were the negative numbers "-1" — "-100," and that line, too, became an arrow after "-100," indicating infinity in the negative numbers pointing to the left.

This was fascinating to me, learning that these numbers never stopped—learning about infinity.

I also learned at an early age about infinity from my mom, who told me God has no beginning and no end. I could easily grasp that God would not die and would go on forever, but how in the world was there no beginning? This is still mind-boggling to me, even though *Conversations with God* says, and science is proving, that time is an illusion here in the Realm of the Physical/Relative. All things really are happening in the eternal moment of now.

I didn't have much experience with death as a child. Thankfully, we had no tragedies in our family until I was in junior high, when my cousin Teddy's beloved grandfather, JoJo, shot himself. This was shocking to all of us kids because he had always seemed so jovial, with a big grin and a twinkle in his eye. When we arrived at the funeral home, Teddy's older sisters and his mom were very worried about Teddy. They pointed out that he was sitting all alone in one of the front pews, and they asked me to go talk to him. "What should I say?" I asked. They said, "Just go sit with him. He's really upset."

I guess I had already figured out by this time that what the churches taught about death and heaven and hell didn't make sense. Because JoJo had taken his own life, the unspoken agreement was that he would be going to hell. I just couldn't believe this to be the case, and my memory is that I told Teddy so. JoJo had been such a good grandfather. We all loved him and there was just no way he was not going to be with God!

Later on, Teddy's family told me I had helped him a lot. I guess it was one of those times when we don't know what to say, but the right words just come.

What I didn't tell Teddy was that I was already questioning whether death really existed at all. It was because the vision of that number line kept coming up in my mind and raising this question: If that long, long line of infinity which runs in both directions represents time, why do we only get to live in one tiny dot on the line? If the timeline of the world is that vast and endless, I wondered, why would we only get to experience such a tiny part of it? And what about babies and children who never reached adulthood? That really seemed unfair!

My seventh grade science teacher was the first to expose me to the idea that maybe we would get more time after all. In hindsight, it's hard to believe he was allowed to teach us about reincarnation in our little town in upper East Tennessee, but without calling it that, that's what he did, by reading to us from *The Search for Bridey Murphy*.

The book told of an American woman who, while under hypnosis, spoke with a thick Irish brogue about her former life as Bridey Murphy in Cork, Ireland. The book was very detailed with the dates of her birth, marriage, and death, names of her family members, information about the Antrim coast, what life was like in those days, and other things that this American woman had no way of knowing. Researchers were able to corroborate most of her story. And under hypnosis as Bridey, she even talked about watching her own funeral, and she said she was confused as to how she ended up as someone else!

I guess my little town was more progressive than one might think because when I told my grandmother, Meme, about that book, she told me she believed that reincarnation was possible. Well, that was all I needed to hear. It made sense to me, and if Meme was cool with it, I was too.

What we have come to know through *Conversations with God* is, not only do we live infinitely in as many different physical forms as we choose, but because there's really no such thing as time, we are living all of these lives *at once*. We travel from the Realm of the Physical, through the Realm of Pure Being, to the Realm of the Absolute, then back again, over and over, and we do this all at the same "time." Talk about mind-boggling!

If we can understand that the Physical Realm is one of illusion, though, all of this can begin to make some sense to our human brains. We think our tangible world is what's real and that when we dream, we are taking a temporary departure from our home, here in the Realm of the Physical. The Toltecs and those of some other faith traditions believe, however, that our *physical* life is the dream, and when we come here, we are taking a temporary departure from our home in the Realm of the Spiritual.

I'm reminded of a round we used to sing on the playground, not realizing how truthful and what good advice it was:

"Row, row, row your boat gently down the stream.
Merrily, merrily, merrily, merrily, life is but a dream."

Okay, so what if the Spiritual Realm truly *is* our home? Why would we choose to continue traveling to the Physical Realm and back, over and over?

Because being in the Realm of the Physical/Relative is the only way to experience contrast, which gives us opportunities to decide who we are in relation to "other" things and what we are going to do about it. And when we allow how we feel to guide us to higher and higher choices, we continue to use this contrast to create greater and greater versions of ourselves.

This process of life is quite elegant, don't you think? Simple, once you get it, yet profound in its implications. Why would we only get to do this once? We'd have an awful lot to accomplish in a very short period of "time," don't you think?!

Please write in your journal or post on the website your answers to the following Self-Reflection Questions:

1. Do you believe you have lived before in a different physical body? Do you have any recollection of this? If so, please explain. Did you come to this conclusion on your own or perhaps while under hypnotic regression?

2. Do you like the idea of coming back into physicality as someone else, or does this idea make you uncomfortable?

3. Do you think you chose an agenda for your life before being born into your current physical form? If so, what do you think it is, and do you think you're fulfilling it? If not, what would it take for you to make that happen?

The following is an Action Step for you to take over the next week:

Read Neale's book, *Home with God: In a Life That Never Ends*. If you've already read it, please read it again. Try hard to commit the "Eighteen Remembrances" to memory so you may use them to comfort yourself and others when loved ones make their transition to the next stage of life.

Postscript

As I write this, today is Good Friday, the beginning of Easter weekend. I knew upon awakening this morning that today is the perfect day to write the Postscript for the chapter, "Death does not exist."

One week ago, I woke up to the news that my mother's beloved, Ed, had passed. I had just arrived in Medford, Oregon the evening before, to be with Neale and the team for eight days, first at our annual No-fee Retreat, followed by more in-depth training in the CWG Messengers School. When I turned on my phone, I was shocked to hear Mom's message that Ed had died the night before on their thirteenth anniversary, St. Patrick's Day.

Knowing that all three of us daughters lived out of town and she had no one there to support her, my first instinct was to rush to her side. When I called her to ask if she wanted me to come, she sounded so vulnerable in her reply, "Oh, would you?! That would be so wonderful." I said, "I'm there. I'll be back in touch when I get my flights."

This is when the miracles began. Medford has a very small airport in southern Oregon, and Mom lives in Knoxville, a mid-sized town in East Tennessee whose airport isn't much bigger. After checking flights online and finding nothing that wasn't exorbitantly expensive, I started calling several different airlines. Not only was I not getting any help from bereavement fares as they rarely exist anymore, I also wasn't finding a way to get to Knoxville any time soon. Eventually, I got an American Airlines representative on the phone who took it upon herself to help get me there fast. She informed me that because Medford is so small and it was spring break, there was only *one seat* on any plane out of there the next three days. It would be that afternoon, and it was going to Seattle. She said there were no seats on any planes out of Medford on either Saturday or Sunday, so if I wanted to get to

Mom quickly, I'd better grab the last seat on that flight to Seattle before someone else did. We would tackle the rest of the itinerary afterward. I said, "Okay, let's do it."

The second miracle came when I found there was only *one seat* that night on any flight out of Seattle that could get me to a connection for Knoxville the following morning. This happened to be a red eye to Atlanta. She said I could get a hotel in Seattle and fly the next day to save a few hundred dollars, but if I did that, the soonest I could get to Mom would be 8:30 pm the next night. It didn't take long to nix that idea as the whole point was to fly to her side right away. Knowing "there's more where that came from," financially speaking, I decided to grab it and go.

The third miracle happened the next morning. After sleeping surprisingly well the whole way from Seattle to Atlanta (sandwiched in the middle seat in the back of the plane between two ginormous men!) I was walking to my gate expecting a three hour layover for my Delta connection to Knoxville at 10:00 am. On the way to my gate, I passed another gate whose notification board indicated an earlier flight to Knoxville at 9:00 am. Hmmmm . . . I wondered why this flight had not been offered to me when booking my trip, so I found a Delta help desk (a miracle in itself!) and inquired about it. It just so happened this was *an extra flight*, added due to a cancelled flight to Knoxville the night before. The agent said there was plenty of room on it and I could take it for no extra charge. She said she wasn't sure if my bag would get there, but that *I* would! She gave me a new boarding pass, and I went back to that gate just as they were bringing breakfast for everyone who had been inconvenienced the night before. Nice! It was a beautiful new plane with hardly anyone on it, and the friendly flight attendant served free Bloody Marys to anyone who wanted them, again to assuage the aggravation of all the people who'd had to unexpectedly spend the previous night in Atlanta. After all I'd been through, I took her up on it!

So thanks to these miracles, I made it cross country to be with my mom the morning after receiving her distraught phone call, instead of three days later. Of all three of us daughters, I had, by far, the longest distance to travel, yet I was the only one who got there right away. We decided to take turns being with Mom, to try to help transition her to getting used to being without Ed, so I got her all to myself.

It's a week I will never forget, with lots of tears, yet lots of laughs; lots of deep discussions, and lots of purging stuff in her condo, all of which are good for the soul. The last miracle of the trip happened after telling her this story from my past:

> Ten years ago, Greg and I met Neale for the first time (that was a miracle in itself, too!) in Milan, Italy, to provide music for his five week European lecture and workshop tour. I grew spiritually by leaps and bounds in those five weeks, so much so that I kind of shocked myself when I got home. I received a phone call from the husband of a hairdresser I knew, Tammy, who was best friends with my long-time hairdresser, Lori. He told me the sad news that Lori had died of sleep apnea while I was overseas and that he was going through her appointment book and found my name, scheduled for a haircut when I got back. Her passing was completely unexpected because she was only thirty-three years old and seemed to be in perfect health. He knew that I had sung at her wedding, so he asked me if I would

sing at her funeral. Although I'd never done the music for a memorial service before, I readily said yes.

I knew right away that I wanted to sing a song I'd recorded, "Say Goodnight," by the great singer/songwriter Beth Nielsen Chapman, written for her husband after his passing. I had sung it while in the Netherlands with Neale the week before and received an unforgettable response from a woman who, in tears of joy, told me she had felt her departed sister's presence while I sang it. She said although they'd been very close, this was the first time since her sister's passing that she had felt her presence, so I knew it was perfect for Lori's memorial service.

As the day drew near, I had a gnawing feeling that I should also say something before I sang. I knew all of her friends from the salon and knew they would be hurting terribly, and I wanted to try to comfort them somehow. As I had just spent the most profoundly life-changing five weeks of my life, I let go of the thought that it "wasn't my place" to say anything and jotted down a few notes that I felt inspired to share. I've never forgotten them. Here's what I said to that room full of Lori's distraught friends and family that day:

"I have good news. Lori is in this room. Lori Martin Powers is in this room, right here, right now. Although you cannot see her, she is here. Because she left us so young, and so beautiful, and so suddenly, I invite you to be open to the possibility that she may give you a sign to let you know she's okay. It could be you'll see something purple, her favorite color. Or maybe you'll get a whiff of her perfume just when you're thinking about her. I invite you to be open to the idea that she is finding a way to let you know she's okay." And with that, I sang the song. How I got through it without crying myself, I'll never know.

I waited a couple of weeks afterward to give Lori's friends some time to grieve, but after nearly two months I really needed a haircut, so I scheduled one with Tammy. I didn't know what I was going to find in that salon. I thought things would be pretty quiet and everyone would still be feeling sad. However, nothing could be further from the truth.

As soon as I walked in, Tammy spotted me from across the room and joyfully exclaimed, "I got my sign! I got my sign!" I was so surprised to see everyone so happy, and said, "That's great! What happened?"

She said that one by one, everyone had gotten a sign from Lori except her. This felt terrible because she was Lori's closest friend. Her sign came at Orlando's "Festival of Trees" when she went with her friend Patti and her kids to decorate Christmas trees. While they were busy decorating, she said my recording of the song "Say Goodnight" came over the loudspeaker. "I knew it was her!" she said. Now, this song was only an album track, not a released single either by Beth or me, and whether Tammy heard Beth's recording or mine, I really don't know because our voices are quite similar. But the fact that it was somehow on the Festival's playlist and then came on at the perfect time, tells me it must have been a miraculous message from Lori.

After relating this story to Mom, I asked her if she had felt Ed's presence since he left. She said simply and sadly, "No." At dinner later, I thought to tell her how the miracles had lined up to get me to Knoxville so quickly, and had they not happened, it would have taken me three days to get to her. It was then that Mom's eyes opened wide in astonishment, and she broke into one of the happiest smiles I've ever seen on her face as she exclaimed, "That's my sign! Oh, Eddie, thank you! That's my sign!"

THE VOICE

Laura (Maitland, Florida)

This lesson's first *Voice* addendum is a bit different than the others. After sharing the story above with my "soul sister" Laura, she reminded me of the powerful messages she received from both her mother and father after their passing, a number of years apart. Although these weren't spoken by *The Voice* as dictated to people in the other chapters, they were, nevertheless, signs from the Realm of the Spiritual. And though they came from the souls Laura knew so lovingly as "Mom" and "Dad," they are still messages from *The Voice*, just in another form because, as we learned in Chapter 1, Lesson #1, "We are all One." If these "after death" messages from the dearly departed aren't God's way of comforting us in times of grief, I don't know what is. Here's what happened, in Laura's own words:

My mom was beautiful, funny, witty, brilliant, a little vulnerable, yet determined enough to stand up for herself. She was the ultimate protector and champion of her children. She was my love, my best friend, and the very heart of our family. When we lost her there was a tremendous void, not only in our lives, but it felt to me as though the whole world had shifted on its axis. This world would never be the same again without her in it.

I lost my mom to a massive heart attack that came without warning. She was here one day, then after two days of swift decline, she was gone. I was left with a huge sense of loss and confusion. Having watched her struggle and suffer for two days and having witnessed her being ripped from life so quickly, I felt an overwhelming need to know she was okay. I probably cried every day for weeks.

Late one night I stood in front of the fireplace, watching the last embers burn themselves out. I was crying and thinking about how terrible those last days had been for her. I just wanted to know she was okay. I prayed. I prayed hard, with tears running down my face, and with the same thought, over and over. Is she okay? I just have to know she is okay. Please God, just let me know if she is okay.

Exhausted, I finally headed to bed, but first went down the hall past my bedroom to turn out a light in the front room. As I walked down the hall my sweet cat Sierra walked past me, brushing up against me. As I passed her I reached down to give her a pet and ran my hand all the way to the tip of her tail. There was a piece of paper lightly stuck to the end of her tail, which I pulled off and dropped to the floor.

I remember thinking how odd that was. What paper could be stuck to her tail? I walked back and picked it up. It was a sticker from the pot of yellow mums I had brought to the hospital for my mom. A sticker the hospital had put on it to identify whose it was. A sticker that had been on the pot when I brought it home. A sticker I had thrown away a month earlier. And on it was written my mom's name and the date of her birth. At that moment, as I stood there with it in my hand, I had my answer. Mom is safe. Mom is okay.

As I was growing up, my dad was tough on us kids. He was determined to keep us "in line" and have us do as he said. I know that sounds harsh, but I believe his huge sense of responsibility for our well-being at times resulted in our feelings of resentment. Don't let Dad know when we did something stupid or wrong, or we would hear all about what we should have done or not done and the better choices we could have made. But as we grew older we learned that he was always there for us, in whatever difficulty we encountered. And as he grew older his demeanor softened. He was always there to give guidance, to protect and care for us.

My dad loved to have fun. We had great family vacations at least twice a year that included camping on Okracoke Island in North Carolina and long trips from our home in Virginia to sunny Florida over Christmas vacation. He loved to embarrass us by dancing a jig in public, speaking to strangers, even giving them advice. When meeting our friends he would turn his glasses upside down and put a red ball on the end of his nose he had fashioned from a ping pong ball. Dad was pretty healthy and active most of his life, riding his bike around the neighborhood almost daily. He ate mostly unprocessed food and had few vices. He even remarried at 89, over a decade after losing my mom.

At 90 he was diagnosed with hairy cell leukemia. At 91, with a compromised immune system, he developed pneumonia. His weakened body just couldn't fight it off. One morning he announced that he was tired of fighting and was ready to go. Just like that. Over the next few days, we gathered around him in the evenings, telling stories, sipping wine together, cooking meals, and having our last private conversations with our dad. He asked us each to look out for each other and to take care of our stepmom.

Not knowing how long Dad would be with us, I went back to work teaching, expecting a call that could come at any time. When the call came, I dashed to my car to drive to my dad's home, almost thirty miles away. Even though I knew my dad had already passed, I felt a sense of urgency to get there as quickly as I could. I was headed east, driving well over the highway speed limit, feeling all kinds of sadness and a mix of emotions. I looked down at the speedometer and noticed the rim of the dial was glowing with a lovely iridescent blue.

Blue was my dad's favorite color. I couldn't see a source for the light—the sun wasn't low enough to cause that to happen, and I had never seen it glow before. So I simply concluded it was probably Dad telling me to slow down. "No need to hurry. Get there safely." That would have been his advice. "Yes, Dad, I'll slow down."

As I merged onto another highway, now driving to the north, I started speeding again. I just wanted to get there as quickly as I could. Again I looked down at the speedometer, and there was that glowing blue iridescence! Well, now I couldn't blame it on the sun; I was going in a completely different direction. "Yes Dad, you're right. I will slow down and get there safely."

Afterward, while visiting with my dad's Lutheran minister, I told him the story about what had happened on my drive home that day. I told him I felt like Dad was still guiding me, looking out for my well-being. The minister's answer surprised me. He told me how lucky I was to have the awareness to recognize the signs of my dad reaching out to me. He said there are always signs of loved ones reaching out to comfort or guide us. We just have to know to recognize them.

As an addendum to Laura's stories, I want to share an interesting experience that involved her cats, Gus and Beau. When I first met Laura many years ago, she was knocking on our front door, asking if I had any foster kittens for adoption. Apparently word was out in the neighborhood that anyone who wanted a kitten should come see me! She was specifically looking for a long-haired calico female. Since I was between litters at the time, I referred her to the Orlando Humane Society. Sure enough, they had a litter of three tiny three-week old kittens who had been dropped off without their mother, and one was a calico female. Since they needed a foster home, she agreed to take them with the intent of keeping the two females when they were old enough to be adopted.

She found a wonderful home for the male, who she named Gus, with her close friends who lived right across the street. It sounded like the perfect "have your cake and eat it, too" scenario, as she would be able to visit him as much as she liked. As the time drew near for her to give him up, however, she found herself completely torn up about it. While raising him for so many weeks, she had made a deep soul connection with him. Her friends, of course, understood, so Laura kept all three of the kittens, and they became part of her family for many years.

Gus was the first to leave her, after succumbing to a very large tumor on his shoulder. Over the next few years, his sisters passed on as well, eventually leaving Laura cat-less. After giving herself time to grieve, she decided it was time to look for a new cat to adopt. She made a number of visits to see rescued kitties but just wasn't finding one she felt a connection with—that is, until she was undeniably drawn to a gorgeous male Maine coon named Beau.

When she brought him home she was amazed at how comfortable he seemed as he walked around the house like he knew the place, and even more at how he would go to the very spot in the backyard where Gus loved to bask in the sunshine. There were so many similarities, she kept accidentally calling him Gus, even though Beau looked completely different. Eventually, she had a consultation with our animal communicator friend, Kate Solisti, the author of *Conversations with Cat*, *Conversations with Dog*, and *Conversations with Horse*. When Kate saw the photo of Beau, she immediately said, "You know he is special. He is an old friend." When Laura told Kate of the similarities in behavior between Beau and Gus, Kate matter-of-factly said, "Beau *is* Gus." This felt so true to Laura, she burst into happy tears.

She and I were discussing this one day, and I asked her, "How in the world could it happen that Gus came back to you? Think of all the miracles that had to line up to make that happen. The odds against it are extraordinary. Do you think it's because the world is more illusory than we think it is?" Laura paused for a moment, stared into space, then replied, "I think I'm getting an answer." I said, "Write it down right now!" This is what she heard:

If I can do something so complicated as putting together a human body, what is so difficult about bringing two souls together?

Annie (Los Angeles, California)

At the time of this writing, a huge fire is burning out of control just north of us in Los Angeles County. We saw the smoke and flames from our rooftop night before last when it started, and the speed and breadth with which it's spread has been alarming. I always have great concern for the animals trapped in wildfires and found that by yesterday morning, I felt sad and completely off-center, so I went within for wisdom from my inner *Voice*:

This is the perfect way to feel better when you don't feel happy. It's really good you catch it so quickly. Work to see if you can shorten the times of misalignment. Meditate more. Focus on Mother Nature more, really seeing each creature for its wonderful magnificence. Yet know that all who pass into this world pass out of it. If you did not want to do so, you wouldn't come in in the first place. The time and place of each exit is perfect and chosen by each soul, so don't be too sad about the fires. They are perfect, or they wouldn't be happening. Just send your love to all of the souls impacted by it. See them as easily slipping out of the Maya of physical existence back into the Ultimate Reality whence they came. That is, indeed, a momentously joyous occasion! It's all good, I promise. It's all good because it's all God. It's truly all God, and I don't make mistakes. Trust that whenever you get blue.

Chapter 4

LARGER UNDERSTANDINGS

Chapter 4, Lesson #1

Welcome to the first lesson in Chapter #4. In the next four weeks we will be working to gain "Larger Understandings" of some of the more complicated concepts in the *Conversations with God* material.

I must admit, I'll be gaining more understanding also, because you teach what you have to learn. Actually, according to CWG, we don't really "learn" anything because at the soul level we already know all there is to know. What we're really doing here is going through a process of remembering mentally what we already know spiritually, so let's see what we can remember together about some of these more complicated concepts. We'll start with what is, to me, the most challenging one to fully understand:

**THERE IS NO SUCH THING AS TIME AND SPACE;
THERE IS ONLY HERE AND NOW .**

How does this concept feel for you? Do you also have a bit of trouble really grokking this one?!

I can pretty much get that time is an illusion, but I have a hard time wrapping my head around the idea of space being an illusion, too. But since we know from science that time and space are fundamentally intertwined, I'm going on faith that this is true, and I believe I will have a "larger understanding" of it as we move through this lesson together.

What *is* time, really, except for the interval of movement from one place to another, here in the Realm of the Physical? As Wikipedia says, "Many experiments have confirmed time dilation, such as atomic clocks onboard a Space Shuttle running slower than synchronized Earth-bound inertial clocks, and the relativistic decay of muons from cosmic ray showers. The duration of time can therefore vary for various events and various reference frames."

That's a mouthful that states scientifically what we feel intrinsically. We know from our own experience that sometimes time seems to speed up, and sometimes time seems to move really slowly. It's just our perception of how quickly or how slowly things seem to be happening.

When I was growing up, our family always went to Myrtle Beach, South Carolina, the third week in August. What a lucky little girl I was, to have a wonderful vacation like that to look forward to, and to enjoy every year! I loved it so much I always made a conscious decision to make every moment count. I would sit on the sea wall each evening before dinner, gaze at the ocean, and count how many days I had left. In that way, I was able to really stretch out the week. "I have seven whole days!" I would say to myself the first evening. The next evening I'd say, "I have six whole days left!" Then the next evening, five, then four, then three, then . . . "Uh-oh, I only have two days left. I need to remember to make each moment count." Then, sadly, "Oh, I only have one day left. I'm going to cherish every minute."

And I did. Those last days at the beach, I would wake with that knowingness and keep it close. As a result, they felt nice and long because I was being fully present—keeping my focus in the "here and now" much more than normal. What would life be like if each of us, as adults, made a conscious decision to do this every single day, all day long? Think we would get more enjoyment out of life? Think we would appreciate it more?

As *Home with God* says, "There are more possibilities in every moment within every lifetime than you might previously have imagined."

Now, what about the part of this lesson's concept that says there is no such thing as space? What is *Conversations with God* trying to convey to us with this message? I think it is telling us the way things really are in the Realm of the Absolute, and that is where we'll have a full understanding of its truth: "For in the Realm of the Spiritual, all things exist in their absolute form. There is only absolute Love. There is only Here, and only Now."

The illusion of space means nothing to the soul in the Spiritual Realm, which can be wherever it wants to be the moment it chooses it. The trick is to learn to use this while here in the body, and there are reportedly yogis in India who can. I've read that some can even *bilocate*—they've been known to appear in two places at the same time! How is that humanly *possible*, you might ask? I think it's because these yogis spend countless hours over countless years in such deep communion with the Divine, they eventually embody It, which allows them to manifest mind over matter.

I've always wished I could twitch my nose like Samantha in the TV show *Bewitched* and be wherever I want to be in an instant. Nowadays, though, we have the next best thing with Skype and FaceTime. Soldier fathers in foreign lands can tell bedtime stories to their wee ones here in America and even be in the delivery room when their wives are bearing their children. CNN produced a story about this, and the commentator off-handedly asked, "Won't it really be something when we can do this with holographs?" I would take it a step further and ask, "Won't it really be something when we can do this with our thoughts?!" This seems to be possible, as the yogis and others have demonstrated, and as we become more evolved as a species, more and more of us will be able to use the knowledge that space is an illusion in a practical way.

My friend Rusty, a gifted cranio-sacral therapist, has found a way to manipulate time and space that works for him when he's driving to work. He used to have unpleasant commutes to his office each morning because the route takes him through numerous traffic lights. He didn't like having to stop at so many red lights, so one day he decided to create something different. He started affirming each morning as he got into his car, this mantra: "I am in harmony with time and travel. I am in harmony with time and travel." Guess what? He stopped catching all those red lights. He gets so many green lights now, his daughters take them for granted. They complain to Rusty that they don't like riding in the car with their friends' parents because they have to sit through too many red lights!

Why do you suppose that works for him? Likely, it's because he not only knows his own power; he also knows there is fluidity in the space/time continuum. When Rusty states his intention with conviction, the Universe reflects back the perfect people, places, and events to make his drive a pleasant and safe one.

Home with God goes on to say, "You are making continuous journeys through the space/time continuum, endless in number," and "You remain *Now Here* for all eternity. 'Now Here' is the only Time and Space there is."

My intent in writing these lessons is to make these Core Concepts from CWG functional in our lives, and my main take-away from this lesson is the reminder to stay focused in, and appreciative of, the present moment because that's really all we have: here and now. When we're aware that time is an illusion, our perceived lack of it becomes a non-issue for us.

Please write in your journal or post on the website your answers to the following Self-Reflection Questions:

1. Have you ever had a moment (or moments) in your life when time seemed to just stand still? If so, what was the circumstance or event that caused that to happen for you?

2. Have you experienced periods in your life that seemed to move more slowly than others? Please explain.

3. Have you experienced periods in your life that seemed to move more quickly than others? Please explain.

The following are Action Steps for you to take over the next week:

Look very closely at how you manage your time. Do you usually feel you have a number of tasks hanging over your head that you just can't find the time to do? Do these unfinished tasks make it difficult for you to fully enjoy the present?

Let's work together here to "clean your plate," so you can begin to really love the present moments of your life. Here are some suggestions how:

Look at each task to see if you really want to do it or if it's something you feel you "should" do.

1. If it's something you feel you "should" do, why, and for whom? For yourself or for someone else?

If it's for someone else and you really don't want to do it, can you find a loving way to tell that person? *Conversations with God, Book 2* says, "Betrayal of yourself in order not to betray another is betrayal nonetheless. It is the highest betrayal." And *Happier Than God* says, "Speak your truth as soon as you know it, but soothe your words with peace."

2. If it's something you really want to do, either schedule it, or go ahead and knock it out!

3. It's a very freeing feeling to get caught up on things in your life. Use a computer calendar program to schedule your "to do list," spreading your tasks out so you can see a way to catch up on them, so they don't weigh

you down. If you don't get to the task on the day you scheduled it, no big deal. Simply move that task forward to another day. If you don't get to it that day, move it again.

Notice, however, if there is a certain task that keeps getting postponed. This may be something you'll want to re-examine to see if you really want to do it. If you decide you don't, just hit the delete button and forget about it! Give yourself the freedom to change your mind because, as we learned in Chapter 1, Lesson #3, "There is nothing you have to do." Life's moments are too precious to not enjoy them, and we don't want to look back on how we spent them with regret.

4. If you feel overwhelmed with activities that you want to accomplish but can't see a way to fit them all in, thank God in advance for helping you manage your time. As in the example above of how the Universe lines up the perfect people, places, and events for Rusty to have a safe and pleasant commute in traffic, state your intention, then allow help to arrive for you in unexpected ways.

5. Do you spend a lot of time "past-urizing" or "future-izing"—in other words, living in the past or projecting into the future? Begin to notice when you do this, then consciously put your focus on the present moment. Breathe into the now and just be.

6. Five times every day, stop whatever you're doing and close your eyes, go within, and be fully present for half a minute. You may be quite surprised at how good this feels! This is what Neale calls "Stopping Meditation." It can be difficult for us to fully appreciate our lives when we're on the go all the time. This simple exercise re-centers us and helps us stay in our good-feeling place throughout the day.

7. Practice "stretching" your present moment to see if you can make it feel like it lasts longer. Then, when you are in a situation that feels especially good, remember to make each moment count. Drink in the deliciousness of the moment at a very deep level so that it is not a fleeting experience for you, but rather, a truly fulfilling one with lasting joy.

Over the next week, please write in your journal or post on the website how these Action Steps are working for you.

Postscript

There is no space, but there's a place. My only place is here, and my only time is now . . . What we choose to do with this time and place is up to us. Are we squandering it or using it wisely? Are we taking for granted that we will be here tomorrow, or are we living each day as if it were our last? One need only look to current events in the news to notice how suddenly we can leave this Earth, sometimes just when we're really getting into the swing of things! This isn't to say for one minute that I think any soul leaves the body before it's ready. This *is* to say, however, that many, if not most of us, leave the body before our *minds* are ready.

What would your present time and place look like if you knew you only had one month to live? If you knew with one hundred percent certainty that in thirty days you would be departing from everyone you know and love, would you change how and where you spend your time? Would you look at some items on your bucket list and say, "Oh, the hell with it!" and just *go* for it?! Could you possibly begin to live like you were dying? If not now, when? If not here, where?

THE VOICE

PJ (Las Vegas, Nevada)

Time is a human construct. People forget that they invent things and then give those things power over themselves. Then they resist the power they think it has over them. They resist what is, which keeps what is, in place.

Sophie (Boulogne, France)

Q: Dear God, could you please tell me more about living in the here and now?

Dear child, you live in an eternal present. Nothing else exists but the moment you're in, right now. The past is gone and cannot be relived; the future is shapeshifting.

Q: You mean nothing is determined in advance?

Before birth, your soul made choices so as to experience what it needed to evolve. Those choices were like broad outlines in a drawing. The details can always change; the colors too. You're free to paint it all red, or blue, or use a much wider spectrum. You're free to enlarge the frame . . .

Q: Hold it! You mean my life can be bigger than it was meant to be?

It was never meant to be a precise shape, or size, or even length. It is what you make it, choice after choice, according to your goals. What can help you make new choices is simply listening to your body and observing your thoughts and feelings. Doing this every day is living in the here and now, while using the past to your advantage (as a tool of measurement and comparison) and the future as a steering wheel (a tool of creation).

So back to your original question. The choice you make in the here and now can change everything, and the beauty of it is that there is a new opportunity every minute!

Chapter 4, Lesson #2

I have a confession to make: After writing the first twelve lessons very quickly, my muse has been strangely quiet for several months. I use the word "strange" because I've absolutely loved writing these lessons! So why the big standstill? I've been blaming it on feeling good about being halfway done, launching the online school, and being busy doing other things, but I finally realized the real reason: I've been putting off writing the lessons for this "Larger Understandings" chapter because the concepts are so advanced I'm having a hard time proving them. I mentioned this to my husband, and genius that he is, he said, "Well, you can't prove we're all One." And that was our very first lesson!

Dear readers, I can only present to you my own ideas about these spiritual messages and try to come up with ways to help you use them. It's ultimately up to you to decide if you agree with the 25 Core Concepts from *Conversations with God*. Neale and I would never want you to accept these concepts on face value, anyway. Diving in deep and arriving at your own conclusions is the only way to get to your truth about anything, so I hope you've been doing that in these lessons.

So, with that understanding, let's move on, shall we? The concept we're going to examine in today's lesson is one that many people in the world would not agree with because it is a highly advanced spiritual principle that takes a great deal of soul-searching to understand:

THERE ARE NO VICTIMS AND NO VILLAINS.

Do you agree with this statement? Would you say that you were ever a victim in your life? Would you say that you were ever a villain in your life? Examining these questions on a personal level is the only way I can prove this concept to myself because to call anyone else a victim or a villain would require me to judge a situation in which I am not privy to all the information there is to know about it.

Some people would say I was a victim of child abuse because I frequently endured harsh corporal punishment from my mom right up until I graduated from high school. But guess what? I never felt like a victim, and it never occurred to me to think of myself as one. Of course I hated getting those whippings, but at least it was punishment that passed quickly, and when it was over I just moved on to my otherwise happy childhood. And thank God, I was only eighteen when Mom and I came to a complete understanding about why it happened, so I didn't have to carry around the negativity of hating her for the rest of my life. On the contrary, I know that had I gone through the things she went through, I very likely would have acted the same way. And since then, my sweet mom hasn't missed one single opportunity to tell me how much she loves me. Talk about a happy ending!

I was also physically abused by my first husband, so some people would say I was a victim of spousal abuse too, but guess what? I've never thought of myself as a victim in that situation either. What happened is just what happened, and thankfully, I had the courage to get out of the marriage quickly. Ironically, it was Mom who rescued me from it. She told me it was totally okay to leave him and file for divorce, and she even gave me a safe haven, allowing me the time and distance I needed to recuperate from such a trying situation.

So these were the two worst things that ever happened to me, and I didn't feel like a victim in either case.

Do I feel that my mom or ex were villains? At the time of all that unpleasantness, I probably did villainize them, but as I gained larger understandings, I dropped those thoughts about both of them. If there are no victims, there are no villains.

But what about the people in this world who *do* think of themselves as victims? I've seen Neale work one-on-one with many people at his retreats and workshops who feel they were victims of something terrible—until he helps them arrive at a larger understanding of what happened. He helps them look at the events from their soul's perspective, often times intuitively. You wouldn't believe the transformation in these people. It's obvious that a huge weight is lifted from their minds when they see what happened from their soul's larger point of view, and it's even noticeable in their bodies—their countenances radiate newfound joy!

In order to embrace the idea that there are no victims and no villains, it helps to remember that we are three-part beings: mind, body, and soul. The following ideas came to me from my inner *Voice* in the wee hours of the morning. They helped me fully understand this concept, and I hope they'll help you, too:

1. *The Mind is not always aware of the soul's agenda.*

2. *There are two purposes for experiencing difficult events/challenges: growth and opportunity.*

3. *The soul is the larger God part of us and is always joyful, loving, accepting, blessing, and grateful (the Five Attitudes of God).*

4. *The soul cannot be wounded.*

5. *Nothing can happen to the soul against its will.*

Think of the Realm of the Physical as a stage on which we get to play out and experience all sorts of roles, and think of the Realm of the Absolute as the place where we set it all up. Before we came here we chose to co-create with others, sometimes willingly assuming the role of "victim" or "villain," in order to assist in our and others' growth through the physical experience. Remember, on the other side we can *know* something about ourselves, but we can't *experience* it. We must come into physicality to do that.

I propose that any thought of one's self as a victim or a villain is a result of incorrect thinking. In order to see the perfection of events, we must move beyond the mind's perspective and try to see it from the soul's point of view. Perhaps this prayer will help:

"Thank you, God, for helping me see through the lens of my soul, rather than the filters of my mind."

Please write in your journal or post on the website your answers to the following Self-Reflection Questions:

1. Is there anything that happened in your past that caused you to feel you were a victim at the time, but now you see a gift in the experience? If so, what caused you to change your mind about it?

2. What is the worst thing that ever happened to you, and do you feel you were a victim? If so, can you try to process what happened in a larger, broader way?

3. What is the worst thing you ever did to someone else? Do you feel you were a villain? If so, can you try to process what happened in a larger, broader way?

The following is an Action Step for you to take over the next week:

This may necessitate getting out of your comfort zone a bit: Have a talk with three people you know who have gone through a challenging event in their lives. It could be a serious illness or accident, loss of a child, physical or sexual abuse, or anything very difficult. Ask them if they feel they were a victim as a result of what happened. If there was another person involved, ask them if they feel that person was a villain.

If they feel victimized or if they villainize another, please be accepting of their feelings. Be gentle and caring, and thank them for sharing their experience. If they imply that they would like to explore a way to get past those feelings, be open to speaking your truth as you are guided to do so, making sure you come from love.

Before each conversation, set an intention for clarity and mutually beneficial communication, and thank God in advance for giving you the perfect words to say if called upon to help that person.

Please write about these conversations and experiences in your journal or on the website.

Postscript

Perhaps the most challenging clients I work with as a Conversations with God Life Coach are the people who are "stuck in their stories." They endured extreme challenges or even horrific ordeals as children that caused them to feel victimized at the time. As they never gained clarity about why it happened, they continue to relive the old memories over and over, often to the detriment of not only their peace of mind, but their physical condition as well. The mind-body link is much more powerful than most of us realize, and these people literally worry themselves sick. In nearly every case, they have at least one person from their childhood who they feel was a villain, and there has been incomplete forgiveness and understanding as to how that person could have done what they did.

While working with one such client recently, I felt inspired to have her write down these words regarding her situation:

"If I am holding the thought that given the exact same circumstances I wouldn't have done the same thing, I am mistaken."

I know we are each unique expressions of the Divine, imbued with our own personalities and proclivities, yet if any of us were to experience 100% of someone else's experiences, I believe it's possible we would make the same choices. As Elisabeth Kübler-Ross said, "There's a little bit of Hitler in all of us."

Maya Angelou also said, "When we know better, we do better." When we come into the world as babies we aren't given a handbook of how to do this thing called life. We all stumble and fall as we're learning our way, and we do the best we can given the circumstances our souls have called forth.

I know there have been plenty of times I've hurt others with my actions and words. I sincerely hope the apologies and amends I've made along the way have been enough to keep them from dwelling on my "mistakes" for the rest of their lives! I offer the gift of understanding, compassion and forgiveness to those who have hurt me, and I pray it's reciprocated.

THE VOICE

Audrey (Sausset-les-Pins, France)

In life, it is quite common to observe within ourselves and/or in others a side which feels like a villain and/or a victim. It is down to us to see through the illusion. Villains and victims are linked by—if I dare say—a karmic link which is a reflection of the cause/consequence of universal law. What if the victim had been a villain? What if the villain had been a victim? What if the victim becomes a villain? Or what if the villain becomes a victim? It is starting to make more sense now . . .

One reaps what one sows, one way or the other, sooner or later.

Wisdom is the middle way. How could one identify this middle path if one does not explore both extremes? Then, finally, one finds the middle way and tunes in with the middle wave. The victim and the villain are each an extremity of this wavelength of which the middle is wise.

Chapter 4, Lesson #3

The concept we're going to examine in today's lesson may be the most perplexing statement in the entire Conversations with God Cosmology:

THE MOMENT YOU DECLARE ANYTHING,
EVERYTHING UNLIKE IT WILL COME INTO THE SPACE.

This is what Neale calls the Law of Opposites, the second step in the Process of Personal Creation from *Happier Than God*. What most students of our teaching don't realize, though, is that this idea of opposing forces has been around for a very long time.

According to Wikipedia (what would we do without Wiki!), the German philosopher, Georg Wilhelm Hegel, pointed out in the 16th century, "Contradiction in nature is the root of all motion and of all life." Karl Marx and Friedrich Engels developed this idea, observing that everything in existence is a combination or unity of opposites. I like this idea of a *unity* of opposites because we know from CWG that "We are all One" (our very first concept).

In traditional Asian philosophy, the concept of Yin Yang is used to describe how polar opposites are actually interconnected and how each gives rise to the other. Heraclitus, a Greek philosopher who lived in 500 BC, not only believed in the unity of opposites, but also that the succession of opposites is a basis for change. In other words, when everything changes, change everything. Hmmm . . . Sounds like a good idea for a book . . . and a song!

Okay, so that's some interesting background, but what about the practical implications of the Law of Opposites? How can we actually *use* it to create a better life?

I think the most important thing to understand about the Law of Opposites is that it's not necessarily a *creative* law. This was pointed out to me by Will Richardson, President of the Board of Trustees of the Conversations with God Foundation, on one of our weekly coaching calls for Neale's Spiritual Mentoring Program (which I highly recommend, by the way).

What I've found while working with people in the mentoring program and others who study the CWG material is, sometimes they are fearful about today's concept, "The moment you declare anything, everything unlike it will come into the space." They become afraid to declare *anything* for fear of attracting the opposite of what they want. They sometimes even go one step further and say, "Well, I'll just declare what I *don't* want, so that its opposite will manifest for me."

Friends, I am here to tell ya, that is *not* how this concept is meant to be interpreted and used!

When we declare something, here's what happens: Our awareness that its opposite *already exists* becomes apparent to us. This is because if we aren't aware of the opposite of what we declare, we cannot experience that which we *do* declare. As *Book 1* states: "In the absence of that which you are not, that which you are . . . is not."

Please note I did not say, "If we don't *experience* the opposite of what we declare, we cannot experience what we do declare." It is enough to simply *know* that the opposite of what we declare exists. We need not experience it first-hand so long as we know of its existence *somewhere*.

Now, if you *do* find that after you declare something, its opposite appears in your experience, or if you're trying to move out of a certain experience but you seem to get more of it for a while, the trick is to not be fooled by appearances. The fact that you're seeing the opposite is life's way of saying, "Notice this thing you *don't* want so that you can better appreciate when you have what you *do* want."

The trick is to not focus too much on the unwanted outcome—don't give it a lot of energy. Just notice it, then stay steadfast in your declaration, keeping your thoughts and feelings positively focused in the direction of your desire. You might even say a prayer of gratitude that goes something like this: "Thank you, God, for showing me what I *don't* want, so that I can know what I *do* want and move more fully into that." Remember, the contrast here in the Realm of the Relative is for our benefit. As long as you don't give up, the undesired experience will begin to disappear.

When we are clear that there is no separation in the Universe—when we can see the Law of Opposites as a *unity* of opposites—we can drop our fear and see so-called opposites for what they really are: varying degrees of one particular thing. Let's look at an illustration of how this might be represented on a scale of degrees:

<— cold...................TEMPERATURE.................... hot —>

<— small..............YOUR BODY SIZE.......................large —>

<— poverty..............YOUR FINANCES..............abundance —>

<— illness ....YOUR PHYSICAL CONDITION............health —>

<— perceived failure............YOUR CAREER...........perceived success —>

<— fear.............YOUR POINT OF ATTRACTION..................love —>

If we are experiencing something we don't want, we can see from this illustration that *its opposite already exists*. If we're experiencing poverty in our finances, we see that abundance already exists. If we're experiencing illness in our physical condition, we see that health already exists. When we fully understand this, we can begin to consciously move in the direction of our desire.

It's interesting to note that these arbitrary opposites have no absolute endings. They continue infinitely on both ends of the scale. For example, when something is as cold as we can measure, absolute zero, its energy continues moving at a quantum level. There is no upper end on the temperature scale that we definitively know of, either. Likewise, when looking through the most powerful telescopes and microscopes in the world, our scientists see that infinity goes in both directions—not just larger and larger, but also smaller and smaller.

When we understand that it is our choice to experience ourselves at any point along these scales, we can begin to use the Law of Opposites for the purpose in which it was intended: as a tool to provide contrast for us. And we use contrast all day, everyday, in matters both important to us and not so important. Here's a little example: I love soy milk cappuccinos in the morning, but if I have them *every* morning, they aren't as special anymore. Too much of a good thing ceases to be such a good thing!

I'd like to make one last point: Today's lesson states that when we declare a particular thing, its opposite will come into the space, but what I think is meant by "the space" is our *awareness*. Thus, today's concept might also read like this: "The moment we declare anything, everything unlike it will come into our awareness." Much like when we buy a particular model of car and we start noticing cars like ours everywhere we go, this law works in the same way. We start to notice things that are both like *and* unlike our stated declaration. We haven't called them into existence. Rather, our awareness of what is already there has simply been heightened.

◇◇

Please write in your journal or post on the website your answers to the following Self-Reflection Questions:

Picture yourself on each of the scales above and answer the following questions:

1. Where are you at this moment on the TEMPERATURE scale? Moving toward cold or hot?

2. Where are you at this moment on the scale called YOUR BODY SIZE? Moving toward small or large?

3. Where are you at this moment on the scale called YOUR FINANCES? Moving toward poverty or abundance?

4. Where are you at this moment on the scale called YOUR PHYSICAL CONDITION? Moving toward illness or health?

5. Where are you at this moment on the scale called YOUR CAREER? Moving toward perceived failure or perceived success?

6. Where are you at this moment on the scale called YOUR POINT OF ATTRACTION? Moving toward fear or love?

What do these answers tell you about yourself? How do you feel about where you are on each of these scales? Please don't judge yourself as "wrong" about any of these positions. Simply observe what is apparently true for you right here, right now.

The following are Action Steps for you to take over the next week:

1. If you found yourself at a place that doesn't feel good to you on any of the scales above, make a conscious decision to start moving in the direction that feels better. Write down your next greatest vision of what that would look like for you. Spend quiet time with your soul each day, allowing inspiration to come through, and take positive-feeling action when guided to do so. Try using these "Seven Steps to Achievement" by Calvin Lehew, entrepreneur, metaphysical teacher, and co-author of *Flying High*:

1) DESIRE: Here's where Neale's Process of Personal Creation starts. You want something that is not apparently present in your life, whether it be a physical thing or a situation.

2) IMAGE: Form a mental image of your desire. Allow yourself to think big by opening up your vision.

3) GOAL: Calvin says the image and goal steps actually overlap: "After you desire something, you form an image of it in your mind's eye and then set it as a goal. Writing it down is important. Refer back to it often." The reason to refer back to it often is because what we focus on expands. We realize it—make it real—more quickly, the more good-feeling thoughts we give it.

4) FAITH AND BELIEF: You must believe that you will have what you desire. This step is even stronger if we can come from CWG's third Level of Awareness, the level of *knowing*. If you see evidence of the opposite of your desire, stay steadfast in your faith and belief, keep your eye on your goal, and know that even before you ask, it is *already* given. This is God's great promise.

5) ACT: I love what Calvin says about this step, that many people in the New Thought community think they can just sit in the lotus position and find gold in their hands. Some yogis reportedly can do this, but most of us aren't there yet! *Inspired* action is what's called for here.

6) GIVE: As CWG says, if there is anything you want in your life, the fastest way to have it is to be the source of it for another. Calvin agrees, saying, "You must give in order to receive. This is a Law of the Universe. In business, you have to give a product or service in order to receive compensation. Likewise, if you want love, you must give love . . . The most successful business is the one that gives the most."

7) RECEIVE: This is perhaps the hardest part of the process for many of us. "There must be no feeling of guilt or unworthiness. If so, there must be forgiveness—either for you or toward others. You must have a good self-image, or you will unconsciously sabotage your goals."

2. Read *Happier Than God*, paying close attention to the chapters that describe the Process of Personal Creation. If you've already read it, please read it again.

◇◇◇

Postscript

I want to expand just a bit on Calvin Lehew's seventh Step to Achievement, as outlined in the Action Step above. When Calvin presents this process to an audience, he has a large placard with a drawing of a ladder on it. Each Step to Achievement is a rung on the ladder, and the seventh and last step, "RECEIVE," is on the highest rung. This seems apropos because without this all-important step, nothing happens. Oh, we will receive *something*, all right, but what that looks like depends not only on our self-image and feelings of worthiness, as Calvin says, but also on staying in our positive frame of mind when the *opposite* of what we want shows up. The choice is to receive on purpose or by default.

I recently re-read Neale's book, *Moments of Grace: When God Touches Our Lives Unexpectedly*. It was published in 2001 and perhaps because it is not included in the Conversations with God Cosmology, it hasn't gotten as much attention as some of his other books. However, it's a hidden gem that I can't recommend highly enough. In it, Neale relates true stories from people who received "immediately answered requests, 'signs' from the heavens," and "things magically falling into place." Some of these people heard God's *Voice*, and they all felt the events had changed their lives for the better.

Following each of the stories in *Moments of Grace*, Neale writes a postscript about it, and in one, he includes the dialogue from one of his CWGs in which he was taught the "Process of Ceiving." No book based on *Conversations with God* would be complete without a *Voice* quote from the brave man who led by example, declaring that such a conversation is possible!

THE VOICE:

Neale (Ashland, Oregon)

"Ceiving" is the process by which you create your personal reality. It goes like this. First, you have an idea. This is an act of pure creation. You create something in your mind. You, quite literally, conceive it. Then, you look at what you have created and you make a judgment about it. You have an opinion about what you have conceived. You take a point of view about what you originally conceived. You, quite literally, perceive it.

Now, it is how you look at what has been created, not what was originally created, that becomes your experience. You quite literally receive it.

What you conceive you perceive, and what you perceive you receive. The process is:

Conception.
Perception.
Reception.

If you stay close to your original idea, what you re-Ceive will be very close to what you con-Ceive. This is where Masters live, and their highest ideas become their grandest reality. Yet you often—too often—see things differently than you first saw them (just as you see yourself differently than you first saw you), because you imagine your first idea too good to be true. You thus move away from your original idea. You can then be fooled about what is true. That is, you can be, quite literally, de-Ceived.

Paramahansa Yogananda (Bihar, India)

This lesson's second *Voice* addendum is an excerpt from *Autobiography of a Yogi* that offers an additional explanation of why the Law of Opposites is so important here in the Realm of the Physical:

One day I entered a cinema house to view a newsreel of the European battlefields. The First World War was still being waged in the West; the newsreel presented the carnage with such realism that I left the theater with a troubled heart.

"Lord," I prayed, "why dost Thou permit such suffering?"

To my intense surprise, an instant answer came in the form of a vision of the actual European battlefields. The scenes, filled with the dead and dying, far surpassed in ferocity any representation of the newsreel.

Look intently!

A gentle *Voice* spoke to my inner consciousness.

You will see that these scenes now being enacted in France are nothing but a play of chiaroscuro. They are the cosmic motion picture, as real and as unreal as the theater newsreel you have just seen—a play within a play.

My heart was still not comforted. The Divine *Voice* went on:

Creation is light and shadow both, else no picture is possible. The good and evil of maya must ever alternate in supremacy. If joy were ceaseless here in this world, would man ever desire another? Without suffering, he scarcely cares to recall that he has forsaken his eternal home. Pain is a prod to remembrance. The way of escape is through wisdom . . .

Chapter 4, Lesson #4

"We hold these *truths* to be self-evident, that all men are created equal, that they are endowed by their Creator with certain unalienable Rights, that among these are Life, Liberty and the pursuit of Happiness."

"Do you swear to tell the *truth*, the whole *truth*, and nothing but the *truth*, so help you God?"

These iconic statements in our history and present day illustrate the enormously high value we Americans place on truth. But when we look at them just a bit more closely, we realize some interesting things:

The first example from the U.S. Declaration of Independence shows that our founding fathers had to discuss and agree on which beliefs they held as true.

The second example is the oath that plaintiffs, defendants, and witnesses must take before they are allowed to testify in a U.S. court of law. Even though they promise to tell the truth, people will often have differing, or even conflicting, testimonies about the same event. They come to different conclusions, or truths about it, because our truth comes from our perspective.

In this last lesson of our Larger Understandings chapter, I am going to challenge you to question everything you believe to be true and to accept nothing on face value. This is because, as today's concept profoundly asserts:

THERE IS NO SUCH THING AS ABSOLUTE TRUTH.
ALL TRUTH IS SUBJECTIVE.

Within this framework there are Five Levels of Truth Telling:

1. Tell your truth to yourself about yourself.

2. Tell your truth to yourself about another.

3. Tell your truth about yourself to another.

4. Tell your truth about another to that other.

5. Tell your truth to everyone about everything.

And this, above all else: Speak your truth, but soothe your words with peace.

The Five Levels of Truth Telling are found in the very opening pages of *Conversations with God, Book 2*, though one very important word has been changed here. The book says,

"Tell *the* truth . . ." and I'm suggesting you "Tell *your* truth . . ." because truth is, indeed, subjective. You can only say what is true for *you* about anything.

I remember being confused when I first read in CWG that there is no such thing as absolute truth. As I pondered this idea in my mind I wondered, "what about the Realm of the Absolute?" Isn't anything absolutely true there? I think the answer is, in the Realm of the Absolute, things just *are*. There is no time and space, so All-That-Is exists in its absolute form without the illusion of relativity. For something to be considered true or not true, it would require something *other than*, and in the Realm of the Absolute, there *is* no other.

Yet here in the Realm of the Physical we certainly have plenty of opportunities to decide what feels true and not true to us. Every day we encounter circumstances and events that give us chances to define and refine our ideas, opinions, and values. That's why the contextual field was created in the first place. Ain't it great?! What a wonderful set-up God made in doing this. The thought process may have gone something like this: "I know, I know!" God exclaimed excitedly. "Since there is no relativity here in Absolute Reality, I'll make up a place where I can go sub-divide myself, forget who I really am, and play with the possibilities. Brilliant! Genius! Wonderful!"

Or perhaps not so wonderful for those parts of God who have gotten so lost in the illusion that they no longer enjoy the game. Not so wonderful for those who have given themselves such challenges that they have been completely fooled by appearances and forgotten who they really are. For those who have built up a story that feels so true for them, by God (!), they're not letting it go. These things that have happened to them (forgetting that they happened *through* them), they believe, are the story of who they are. And when they're stuck in their story, they are robbed of the joy that the illusory Realm of the Relative was meant to be.

Byron Katie has helped countless people turn their lives around by asking the simple question, "Can you absolutely know that it's true?"

When asked to look deeply at the events of their lives to see if their prior judgments are absolutely true, the people she works with invariably come up with the same answer: "No."

◇◇◇

Please write in your journal or post on the website your answers to the following Self-Reflection Questions:

1. Do you have any stories about your life that it would serve you to let go of now? Perhaps some old beliefs or grievances that you've held for a long time that it would free you to drop?

Begin by telling your truth to yourself about yourself. Then deeply question that truth. See if what you've told yourself for a long time is absolutely true. If the story involves another, tell your truth about that other to yourself and see if it's absolutely true. If you arrive at new conclusions, follow the other levels of truth-telling as applicable for healing in each particular situation. And please remember to soothe your words with peace and loving kindness when sharing your truth with others. You might even begin the conversation with, "This is only *my* truth about this . . ."

2. Is there anyone you know who is so stuck in their story that it appears to be negatively impacting their life? What can you learn from their experience?

If you feel guided to do so, can you find a gentle, loving way to be with that person that might help him or her release their story? Without coming from judgment or a "holier-than-thou" attitude, and certainly not proselytizing, just be there for them in a way that a door to healing might open through you. We always want to come from big love when offering spiritual assistance to others.

The following are Action Steps for you to take over the next week:

Since our last lesson's Action Step was quite time-consuming, I'm going to go easy on you with these first two steps—easy on your schedule and easy on the ears—and have you listen to two songs that speak about forgiveness and letting go of our stories. Please do this when you have quiet time to really pay attention to the lyrics.

1. Watch and listen to the music video of one of the finest New Thought songs I've ever heard, "I Believe This Belongs To You." Written by my friends JD Martin, Jan Garrett, and Ester Nicholson, it's beautifully performed by Ester, accompanied by my husband Greg on piano. You'll find the video by searching for its title on YouTube.

2. Listen to "Heart of the Matter" by Don Henley, also available on YouTube or for downloading wherever music is sold.

3. Over the next week, whenever you feel stress or dis-ease, please implement the Five Levels of Truth Telling. Be sure to get to the heart of what feels most true for you as it applies to any situation in your life. For example, you might say, "The truth about my finances is . . ." or "The truth about my relationship is . . ." Then follow the other four levels, again coming from big love.

See if this works to increase your joy and peace, and write about these experiences in your journal or on the website.

Postscript

"Just the facts, ma'am."

Okay, for you TV Land buffs out there, what character made this saying famous, and on what television show? Take a minute to think about it if you like. I'll wait . . .

. . . Okay, so who attributed it to Detective Sergeant Joe Friday from *Dragnet*? Am I the only one? Well, guess what? The joke's on me because that has been my truth for as long as I can remember. I just looked it up on Wikipedia for corroboration, and guess what I found? This little gem: "A common misattributed catchphrase to Friday is 'Just the facts, ma'am.' In fact, Friday never actually said this in an episode, but it was featured in Stan Freberg's works parodying *Dragnet*."

IMDb.com, the Internet Movie Database concurs, setting the record straight with this bit of trivia: "Contrary to popular belief, Joe Friday never said 'Just the facts, ma'am' in any episode."

Well, if this isn't a perfect example of this chapter's concept, I don't know what is. Here I was, all set to write a Postscript about the difference in truth and facts, and I bump up against this irony of ironies. Once again, a deeply held truth I've carried around for *decades* has been disproved. If this isn't true, what else might I be wrong about?!

Just the facts, ma'am. Just the facts . . .

THE VOICE

Sophie (Boulogne, France)

. . . Don't go around preaching that truth as "the" truth, or you'll be back where you started: fighting something instead of proposing another way.

Q: Are you saying there are multiple truths?

I am. In the sense that there is no absolute truth in the face of ever-changing events, people, and times.

It's very hard for my mind to get around this. I guess I'm still not free from the need for certainties.

The mind has its limits and it's okay. The soul knows no boundaries and aims further in terms of goals. Its vision of any given situation is much wider. The mind seeks to protect you and your immediate interests at all times. The soul is braver; more insightful. While in this body you need both, so use them wisely, and remember to trust the soul if you are a truth seeker.

Ah! So there *is* a truth!!!

Sure. There is "your" truth. The one you're living right now. And even that truth isn't absolute, as it is ever-changing—just as you are changing.

Yes. That is what makes life so interesting. My truth is about knowing myself, sharing who I am with others, and speaking my truth. I truly live by this, and I'm glad I do because it has made my life beautiful in many ways. Still, sometimes I find myself stuck. I don't know how to express my truth. I find it contradicts the other person's view on life or that now isn't the right time. I feel bad about this, like I'm hiding things, not being honest enough.

Your truth has many layers. Some of it can be shared universally; some of it is intimate. Some people can be enlightened by it; some could choose to feel hurt. Don't feel bad about knowing when and how to share it. Truth wasn't meant to be flaunted, but to be shared, like a gift that keeps on giving. It takes courage to share it, and wisdom to do it in a way that it can be heard.

THE POWER OF THREES

Chapter 5, Lesson #1

In this chapter titled "The Power of Threes," we'll take a look at four concepts that illustrate that good things come in threes. *Conversations with God, Book 1* lists what it calls the Triune Truths, the three-in-one that is found in all realms of the sublime. These include mind/body/spirit, thought/word/action, knowing/experiencing/being, here/there/the space in-between, and a number of others. CWG wants us to know that duality is an illusion—nothing is so cut-and-dried as to be either this *or* that. The aspects of life can be more accurately described as this, that, *and* the other.

In today's lesson, by putting my own life under candid examination, we're going to look at one way to reconcile the mind/body/spirit aspects of ourselves in order to create a greater whole:

**THE THREE CORE CONCEPTS OF HOLISTIC LIVING ARE:
HONESTY, AWARENESS, AND RESPONSIBILITY.**

After allowing this tenet from CWG to stew in my subconscious for a few days, it became clear that the way to use these three concepts of holistic living is to apply them to every area of our lives.

I then realized where I fall short. This may come as a bit of a surprise to you, my dear readers, who might be thinking I've "got it all together," but it's best that you know there's one particular issue I still deal with . . . and sometimes more, depending on the circumstances! But more about that in a moment.

In the four *big* areas of day-to-day living, I am so grateful that everything *does* feel right to my mind, body, and soul:

1. My *relationship* with my significant other, Greg, is everything I ever wished for in a husband, and more. He is my soul mate, closest confidant, and one of the two greatest gifts in my life. My relationships with my family and friends are happy ones, too. There were some neighbors in Nashville who didn't like me, but I can't do anything about that. I know I did my best in my dealings with them, and what they choose to think about me is really none of my business. I send them loving energy regardless.

2. My *work* is fulfilling and lots of fun. I assist people one-on-one in my online school and as a life coach, I sing and play keyboard in a popular Fleetwood Mac tribute band, and I help Greg with his growing film scoring business. As all true benefits are mutual, I'm as blessed in these endeavors as everyone I'm given the honor to help and work with.

3. Our *home* is where my heart is. Our four cats helped us cement the feeling of belonging after moving from our big dream house in Nashville to a darling little bungalow in Hollywood Hills. It was a huge change, but as time has passed, I find I love it more and more. We were so fortunate to find such a safe, lovely garden spot in one of the largest cities in America!

4. My *health* is perfect, thank God. I take care to exercise my body and feed it healthy, whole foods, and I take vitamins and supplements to make sure I give it the nutrition it needs.

But the one thing I need to be more vigilant about, that this lesson on holistic living caused me to take a good hard look at, is this: I love wine. Especially white wine. And I love it so much I have some most every evening.

I know, I know, *Conversations with God* states very clearly that the human body was not designed to consume alcohol. Believe me, I've read it with more than some minor discomfort several times. I rarely drink hard liquor, but having spent much time living in Europe, especially France, wine is, to Greg and me, what goes with dinner. And, truthfully, I love a good party as much as anyone!

So how do I reconcile my desire to drink wine with my desire to live a holistic life?

1. I have to be *honest* with myself about my drinking. Do I drink too much? How much is too much? Do I have a drinking problem? Who is in control here? Me or the wine?

2. This inquiry—this attempt to be honest with myself—led me to become *aware* of what I'm doing. To not reach for a glass of wine automatically, but to do so out of a thought-out decision that, yes, I now choose to have a glass of wine.

3. There's a caveat that a popular beer includes in their advertising that says, "Drink Responsibly." I learned decades ago that I never want to experience bed spins again, so I never drink enough for that to happen. I also decided that I never want to drink enough to dull my mind or blur my speech. To me, it is very unattractive to see someone drunk, and I know with certainty, that is neither who I am nor who I choose to be. So I must somehow reconcile *responsibility* for doing something that I'd be better off doing less of—if not dropping altogether—with a decision to live my life holistically.

I remember being surprised that CWG says the reason the human body isn't meant to take in alcohol is because it dulls the mind. I would have thought it would say something like, "it kills brain cells" or "it destroys the liver," because we know that too much alcohol isn't good for the body. So if alcohol isn't good for the body or the mind, what about the spirit? Does alcohol affect the spirit? Is that why they *call* it "spirits?!" I think it does, but it can work either positively or negatively. Greg and I feel happy and high on life when we finally sit down with a glass of wine and some fine cheese at the end of the work day. We come together to talk about the events of the day and our dreams of tomorrow, and these quality times cement our relationship and lift our spirits. But some people go in the extreme *other* direction: They become "mean drunks" and it happens in a snap. Is that the spirit or the mind being affected? I don't know, maybe both.

So what about the fact that I drink wine most nights? I don't think I'm an alcoholic because I limit my intake and drink responsibly, and I know I don't have an addictive personality. I easily quit smoking when I went to college, after being a pack-a-day smoker for four years. What I have is a *habit*. Every now and then my soul nudges me, reminding me to keep it in check, because I have big things I've yet to accomplish. As I am a work in progress, I must walk in awareness if I'm to continue becoming the next grandest version of the greatest vision I have about myself. Anything less is not living holistically.

What does holistic living mean, anyway? It means not only realizing that we are three-part beings—mind, body, and soul—but also taking good care of all three of these aspects of ourselves. The whole, when well-cared-for, is greater than the sum of its parts.

◇×◇

Please write in your journal or post on the website your answers to the following Self-Reflection Questions:

Are there any areas of your life that it's time to examine in order to live holistically? What would have to change? Be honest with yourself about the issue or issues, and write out your thought process about it.

The following is an Action Step for you to take over the next week:

Set an intention to be aware of these issues in your life, and make a plan to implement a responsible course of action in order to change them. Please write about your progress in your journal or on the website. You may want to recite the following affirmation to yourself daily as a way to stay on course:

"I am honest with myself, and I am aware, responsible, and intentional." Rest assured that I'll be doing this Action Step, too!

◇◇

Postscript

The timing of my task to write this postscript couldn't be better. And that's, of course, perfect, as I'm a big believer in Divine right timing. I truly feel that to everything there is a season, and things unfold perfectly for us when the time is right.

There's a lot of talk about holistic medicine these days, and I'm glad it's becoming more known because it can be very helpful when traditional modalities don't work. Holistic healing invites us to look at the whole person, not just the body, when something manifests physically as disease. Although recognizing the mind-body connection has become somewhat more mainstream in modern medicine, very few doctors include the spirit in their diagnoses. I'm just coming out of a physical situation in which I had the chance to see for myself how these all fit together.

Five weeks ago Greg and I went car shopping. The lease on our Civic Hybrid was due to expire in a few months, and we didn't want to get another Civic because Honda had decided to stop making the hybrid models. We didn't want to go environmentally back-ward with a gasoline-only car, so we went to a Ford dealership to check out their Fusion plug-in hybrids. Greg test drove it first, then pulled over to the side of the road to switch places so I could drive. I felt rushed to adjust the seat and didn't take the time to get it right, so I operated the gas pedal with my right foot completely off the floorboard. (Have I mentioned I'm vertically challenged, at only 5'0" tall? I could barely reach the pedal!) Even though I didn't drive far, by the time we got back to the dealership, I could hardly walk. With every few steps I took, my right knee popped out of place and buckled beneath me. Nothing like this had ever happened before, so I laughed it off at first, but as it got more and more painful, I realized something was quite wrong, so I stopped walking on it.

The next morning, Greg bought me some crutches and a knee brace. I rested for several days, elevating and icing the knee frequently and taking ibuprofen to help the swelling go down. Still, whenever I'd try to walk, my knee would buckle beneath me, so I had a decision to make: conventional medicine or alternative? Not a difficult deci-sion, really, as some of our closest friends here in LA are our chiropractor and his wife, and a conventional doctor would likely treat the problem with prescription drugs and/or surgery, which for me would be a last resort. Both would likely advise X-rays, so at the advice of our chiropractor I had extensive ones taken, which were inconclusive. MRIs were ordered next, but I did something in-between that took care of the whole thing: I treated the issue holistically.

I am so happy to know about Bonnie Prudden Myotherapy. Bonnie, the author of *Pain Erasure*, was an American physical fitness pioneer whose report to President Eisenhower on the unfitness of American children led to the formation of the President's Council on

Youth Fitness. She later developed her Myotherapy system ("myo" means muscle) which saved the careers of several of my musician friends and family through the years, Greg being one of them. Myotherapy involves systematic trigger point release, combined with corrective exercises.

Very often, pain in the body comes from the muscles, and freeing them up to work naturally eliminates it. I had two Myotherapy sessions and found, much to my surprise, that both of my legs were chock full of trigger points. After the second session my therapist, Diane Dahi, said, "Okay, now try to walk." Even after all that wonderful treatment, my right knee immediately buckled beneath me, giving her the perfect opportunity to see for herself what was happening. She paused for a moment, then said, "Hmmm . . . Let's see if there's something spiritual going on." That idea had never occurred to me, but since a strictly physical treatment wasn't helping, I was certainly open to the idea. She opened a Louise Hay app on her phone, "Heal Your Body, A–Z," and searched for knee issues.

The app serves as a quick-reference guide to probable mental patterns behind different body ailments, and what Diane found shocked me. It said knee issues are caused by being stuck in the ego, too proud to bend. I said, "Well, that doesn't sound like me!" so she searched again. This time, she said nothing, sighed, and handed me her phone to read for myself. I immediately burst into tears. It mentioned things like lack of compassion, pride, and stubbornness. Now I knew what I needed to do. I had been coaching a client whose child abuse issues were bringing up similar ones of my own—issues I thought I had addressed sufficiently when I was eighteen, but now realized I hadn't.

This wasn't my first clue. In 2005 when I traveled to Europe to sing on Neale's lecture and workshop tour, we were having dinner at a restaurant in Copenhagen. This was way before I knew I could have my own CWGs to receive answers from my own inner *Voice*. I asked Neale why animals, who are so innocent, have to suffer so much. My eyes welled up with tears before I could even get the question out because this had been my lifelong biggest concern. I'll never forget the way he looked at me when he quietly asked, "Sweetheart, what in the world happened to you when you were a child?" I was surprised by the question and admitted I had endured physical abuse at the hands of my mother, but that we had reconciled when I was eighteen, and our relationship had been wonderful ever since. He said even though that was the case, I would benefit from inner child therapy. I didn't know what that was, so my mind jumped to visions of being locked in a kids' room, forced to play with toys and screaming—something that would feel really silly! I didn't like that idea, so I only made a few feeble attempts over the years to take Neale's advice.

So here I was, years later, in this situation with my life coaching client. I called her and spoke my truth as kindly and honestly as I could, to temporarily recuse myself as her life coach. I told her I needed to take some time to work through what was coming up for me, and thank goodness, she completely understood. When I shared with her that I'd never done the inner child work Neale had recommended, she said she had a wonderful empathic intuitive therapist who specialized in it. Well, that was all I needed to hear, so I said, "It's time. Please send me her contact info."

The beautiful thing about working with Pamela Beaty, also known as "The Hollywood Sage," was that she did all the inner child work, not me. I didn't have to do anything. She immediately knew that the abuse started when I was only eight months old. It was excessive and it was frequent, and I had almost completely blocked it from my conscious mind. The pain that was released through her was horrifying to hear. My poor inner child had been trapped inside for all these years, with no one hearing her or attempting to heal her pain, least of all, me. Now she was finally being acknowledged. Now I could finally tell her how sorry I was and that she didn't do anything wrong; that Mom was just doing the best she could under the very difficult circumstances she was in. And guess what she told me through Pamela? "I just wanna sing! Hurry! Let's do this! That's my favorite way to play!"

Pamela then asked me if I wanted to know my soul's purpose in coming to the Earth. I jumped at the chance, and sure enough, it corroborated my inner child's message to sing. She said I knew before coming into physicality that I wanted to give love to a lot of people, and singing was a way to do that—to spread the love to many people all at once.

It's funny, at a recent retreat Greg and I attended with Neale, we participated in a process called "Ten Things I Am." You might want to try it because it's very illuminating. Tear a sheet of paper into ten pieces, then write on each piece one thing that you are. It might be your vocation, an avocation, or just a natural state of being. I wear a lot of hats, so mine were Grateful, Actress, Life Coach/Teacher, Sensitive, Fun/Funny, Singer/Songwriter, Author, Helpful, Poet, and Friendly. After we'd filled out our ten things, Neale said, "Throw away the five that are least important to you." Hmmm . . . "Now throw away two more." Ooooh, let's see . . . "Throw away one more." Ouch, this is hard! Then . . . you guessed it. The goal, of course, was to get each of us to choose the one thing that matters most. My last two were Helpful and Singer/Songwriter. I circled Singer since I love it more than songwriting, then focused on my decision. The thought of throwing away Singer immediately brought tears to my eyes, so I knew my answer. As important as I feel it is for my life to be more about everyone whose life I touch than my own, I couldn't bear the thought of never singing again. Now I understand why.

My singing *is* helpful to others, more than I probably ever realized. I'm not just doing it for myself. In fact, without an audience, I really don't sing very much. I've always said, though, give me one person in the room who's really listening, and I will sing my heart out to them! It isn't because I want to show off. Far from it, actually. Way too many times when opportunities arose, I was reluctant to sing for people, before I realized I was withholding my gift when I didn't. Rather, I prefer to sing to an audience because there is a reciprocal energy exchange. I give love through my singing, and people give love back when they are touched by it.

The last thing Pamela did was check in with my knee to see if she could figure out why it was popping out of place. She intuited that the inflexibility was due to a deeper indecisiveness about which way to go in my life. She got a mental image of me, going off in all different directions with no clear vision of where. I would start to go one way, then veer off another way, then another, and another. She said my poor knees just didn't know where in the world to go, so they got rigid, which caused them to pop out every time I would change my mind.

Boy, did this ring true. Like I said, I wear a lot of hats. I've also been in a transition period for the past few years, trying to decide what to do with my life since moving from Nashville to LA. I know that I'm here to play big because my *Voice* has told me so, but to play big at what? As much as I love my CWG work and as important as it is, I know now that singing has to be a big part of my life, too. It's what I was born to do.

And guess what? My knee is great now! I'm already hiking and working out, with a larger focus on using proper body mechanics to keep my knees moving with ease. Interestingly, implementing holistic medicine in healing my knee has brought about clarity of purpose. Now that I am *aware* of my why I came to the planet, I must be *honest* with myself in my choices. What would I love to do now? That's what matters most, and it's a question we all have a *responsibility* to ask ourselves if we don't want to die with our song unsung.

THE VOICE

Annie (Kingston Springs, Tennessee)

I just ran across this CWG dated July 11, 2012. I had forgotten all about it, so of course it's timely to find its wisdom once again. It perfectly set my priorities in order, and this time I shall not forget it.

Q: What did I come here to do?

> *Sing*
> *Teach*
> *Write*
> *Play the piano*
> *Love*

"The Sound of Music"—just listen.

I closed my eyes and listened. I heard a barred owl, closer than ever before. A little while later, I heard a bird sing right behind me. Then I recalled these lyrics from the musical:

The hills are alive with the sound of music
With songs they have sung for a thousand years
The hills fill my heart with the sound of music
My heart wants to sing every song it hears.

My heart wants to beat like the wings of the birds that rise
From the lake to the trees.
My heart wants to sigh like a chime that flies
From a church on a breeze.
To laugh like a brook when it trips and falls
Over stones on its way.
To sing through the night
Like a lark who is learning to pray.

I go to the hills when my heart is lonely
I know I will hear what I've heard before
My heart will be blessed with the sound of music
And I'll sing once more.

Kelly (Long Beach, California)

In part two of this chapter's *Voice* section, my friend Kelly beautifully illus-trates what it can look like to walk in *awareness* of The Voice, to be *honest* with yourself and others about it, and how to take *responsibility* by heeding it. She and her husband John live as holistically as anyone I know, and I'm blessed to call them friends. Here is Kelly's story, in her own words:

Two weeks before we were to leave on an all expense paid, five-star luxury trip to the Canary Islands, I had a disturbing dream about the plane having to make a crash landing in the ocean. In the dream, my husband John landed next to me in the water, and I kept begging him to drown me, so I wouldn't have to face being eaten by sharks. I kept begging and pleading with him until he finally pushed my head under the water. As I felt my spirit leave my body,

I saw the rescue helicopter directly overhead. The jolt of realizing that I had forced my beloved to do the unthinkable, only to realize that I would have been rescued moments later, caused me to wake with a start.

Every morning after that dream, I woke with a tight feeling in my chest like something bad was going to happen. I kept pushing it away as irrational. I am a world traveler who has taken *many* overseas flights, and after all, how often does one get this kind of a trip just given to them? Yet every morning the feeling persisted.

Finally, the day before we were to depart, I said to John, "I just can't shake this feeling that something bad is going to happen, and I haven't been able to distance myself from the very real feeling I felt in the dream." I didn't really believe that the exact thing my dream had shown me was going to happen, but I did feel a profound sense of foreboding. John asked me if I had summoned my Guidance for a sign of whether or not to go, and I realized I hadn't. So I asked out loud, "Show me a sign that is clear and easy for me to understand whether or not to take this trip."

The following morning, nothing had shown up, and we had made our way to the airport and onto the plane. After the last passengers boarded, we sat there for about twenty minutes, and then the pilot came onto the sound system and informed us that there was a technical problem with the navigation, and it would be about fifteen minutes more. More time passed, and the pilot came back on and informed us that the part was being delivered from LA, and they had no idea what time we might actually take off. We were asked to de-plane.

Standing in the airport, I asked my Guides, "Is this the sign?"

John and I were summoned over the sound system in the terminal, and when we spoke to the attendant, we were informed that the delay was going to prevent us from being able to make our connection.

"Is *this* the sign?"

When we ran through all of our options, the only one that made sense to get us to the destination was to travel the following day, so we took that booking and left the airport for home. All the way, I struggled with the notion that I had been shown some really clear signs that this trip was not supposed to happen, and yet, I still couldn't make myself cancel. Finally, when we got home, we sat down, and I shared what was on my heart with John. He agreed that it did seem as though we had received our sign and said he would be okay with calling off the trip.

Now, some folks might think this story ends with some disaster happening to that plane or some other such obvious mishap, but thankfully, that is not what happened. All week long while I was supposed to be in the Canary Islands, I continued to ask, "Where would you have me go? Who would you have me meet? What would you have me hear? What would you have me say?"

It has been an exhilarating time filled with many doors opening and a feeling that anything is possible. I may never know exactly why I was meant to cancel that trip, but I know in my heart it was the right thing to do, and I have no regrets.

Chapter 5, Lesson #2

In our first lesson in "The Power of Threes," we explored the Core Concepts of holistic living: honesty, awareness, and responsibility. In this lesson we're going to explore that second concept—awareness—a bit more, as it applies to the Process of Personal Creation:

THE THREE LEVELS OF AWARENESS ARE:
HOPE, FAITH (OR BELIEF), AND KNOWING.

These three levels of awareness have played a huge part in my experience, and I'll bet if you take some inventory of your own, you'll see that they've played a big part in yours, too. By looking at how hope, faith (belief), and knowing have played out in our past, we can better use them to create a greater tomorrow.

Let's begin with the first level of awareness: hope. When there is something we decide we want for ourselves it nearly always begins with hope, especially if it's a *big* something. "I hope I meet the man of my dreams," or "I hope I can sell my house," or "I hope I can beat this cancer."

I spent a decade chasing the country music stardom brass ring. I remember exactly when the hoping started: As soon as Greg and I returned home from Nashville after recording my first country CD (we lived in Orlando at the time), I thought to myself, "Omigosh, we've just spent $30,000 on this record! I've got to do something with it to try to recoup all that money."

I didn't realize it then, but at that moment, the sheer joy of creating such a wonderfully fulfilling project vanished. In its place was a constant feeling of striving for something that felt just out of reach. I was always hoping something big would happen—a record deal with a large cash advance, a radio hit, or anything that would pay back our investment— and although we did have a number of small successes, the big break never came.

My friends and I were just learning about the Law of Attraction at the time. We would try to use it the best we could with our limited understanding, even going so far as to create mock-up music charts with my songs in the #1 position. I'd tack them up on the fridge and hope for a miracle, but I didn't really believe it would happen. I was stuck at the level of hope, with more than a few doubts lingering in the back of my mind. Because hope is the first level of awareness, it is the least effective in creating what we want, so I didn't see a lot of results. This probably happens to many beginners in the Process of Personal Creation who give up and declare, "This stuff doesn't work."

By continuing my spiritual practice through the years, though, I've been able to raise my awareness of just about everything to the second level—faith—and that's certainly a stronger place to be than hope. If our faith is strong, we believe we can have whatever we choose to call forth.

Still, having faith or belief is not as strong as *knowing* without a shadow of a doubt that something is absolutely going to come to pass—the deep-down feeling, perhaps, that *it's already happened,* and the process is simply playing itself out. CWG says all of us have psychic abilities, and maybe when we have a very strong knowing such as this, that's what is really going on at this third level of awareness.

I remember being perplexed when I was single and would meet couples who had been happily married for many years. I would ask them, "How do you know when you meet the right person?" It would drive me crazy when invariably their responses would be, "You just know." I would ask, "Whaddya mean you just know? What does *that* mean?!" And they'd just smile and repeat the answer, "You just know." Well, guess what? The first night Greg and I went out, we spent three hours talking non-stop. When he took me home and kissed me goodnight, I turned back to look at him as he walked away, knowing something very powerful had taken place. In that moment, he also turned back to look at me with the same thought. We both *knew* something very special and life-changing had just happened!

Perhaps an even more powerful example is when he and I, years later, decided to move from Orlando to Nashville. I knew the second we drove by our dream house that it was meant for us. It felt like every cell in my body started buzzing, and I exclaimed, "That's it! That's it!" We totally hit it off with the lady who was selling the house and agreed to buy it right then and there. We decided not to put a contingency of selling our Orlando house on the sales contract because we didn't want someone else to make a stronger offer. When her husband found out about it, he asked me, "What makes you think you're going to sell your house?" Without skipping a beat, I declared, "Oh, it's gonna sell." I totally *knew* it would, and we got an offer the day after we put the "for sale" sign in the yard.

So the question that arises from today's CWG concept is this: Can we *consciously* raise our awareness from hope to faith (belief) and even into knowing, and if so, how?

Well, let's first be clear that hope is not a bad place to be. It's certainly better than hopelessness! If we have a certain desire we're trying to bring into our life, being hopeful will start moving us in the right direction. But if we can elevate that hope to a stronger, more powerful energy of belief, we'll be a big step closer to manifesting what we want. The way to do this is by deeply examining each doubtful thought that creeps into our consciousness until it ceases to have its illusory form. Look to see if the thought that tells you you can't have it is absolutely true. If the thought causes you to feel bad, guess what? You are out of alignment with your desire.

Our job when trying to manifest something in our lives, whether large or small, is to remain a vibrational match to it. We must pay close attention to our feelings. They are our built-in guidance system, and they will never steer us wrong. The better we get at this, the stronger our faith becomes as we start seeing real results. And as our awareness increases that this really *is* how this stuff works, we move closer and closer to knowing that even before we ask, it has already been given. And that, my friends, is the most powerfully creative place to be.

One caveat needs to be mentioned here, though. If there is something you want to manifest in your life, and you think you'll only be happy when you have it, although you may experience a temporary high when it comes to pass, that happiness will be fleeting at best. Outer things cannot bring inner joy. I know several people who have every luxury they could ever want, yet they are not happy. Please don't make the mistake of putting the "be-do-have" paradigm backward. Choose to be happy first, knowing that real foundational joy comes from within. Then anything we decide to call forth after that is just icing on the cake!

Please write in your journal or post on the website your answers to the following Self-Reflection Questions:

1. Can you think of a time when you *hoped* you would manifest something, either tangible or intangible, but it never came to pass? Do you think your level of awareness had anything to do with why it never happened? Please write about that experience and any new understanding you may now have about it.

2. Can you think of a time when you *knew* you would manifest something, either tangible or intangible, and it did come to pass? Do you believe your level of awareness had anything to do with why it happened? Please write about that experience and any new understandings you may now have about it.

The following is an Action Step for you to take over the next week:

Is there anything you would like to call forth in your life? Look to see which level of awareness about it you currently hold, and see if you can work on your thought processes in order to take it up a notch. If your current level of awareness is hope, work to raise it to belief. If your current level is already belief, work to raise it to knowing. Please write about those thought processes, and as time passes, write again about how they are working for you.

Postscript

A few years years ago, I was blessed to be part of a group meditation led by the spiritual teacher Ram Dass at the Awakened World Film Festival. (If you don't know who he is, you might want to Google him!) We had just viewed a documentary titled *Dying to Know: Ram Dass & Timothy Leary,* and the filmmakers Skyped Ram Dass in to speak with us. There he was on the big screen, larger than life, smiling from ear to ear the whole time. The mantra he slowly repeated over and over in his meditation has never left me:

I AM LOVING AWARENESS.
I AM LOVING AWARENESS.
I AM LOVING AWARENESS.
I AM LOVING AWARENESS.

This simple mantra can be construed in a couple of different ways, depending on whether the word "loving" is interpreted as a verb or as an adjective. When "loving" is used as a verb, the sentence means: I am doing the action called loving, and *what* I'm loving is being in a state of awareness. When "loving" is used as an adjective, the sentence means: I am the thing called awareness, and the *kind* of awareness I am is loving. See the difference? Either way, it was a heartfelt statement of a very high truth for Ram Dass, and I would venture to say, something most everyone in that theater was working toward as well. It felt really good to allow his words to sink deeply into my consciousness.

When I first wrote this lesson on the Three Levels of Awareness, I focused mainly on how hope, faith (belief), and knowing apply to manifesting things we'd like to call forth in our experience. I now think the larger, perhaps more important way to use this Core Concept is with our spirituality in mind. We can allow the different levels to serve as a benchmark for where we are in our process of conscious re-unification with the Divine. Do I just *hope* there is a thing called God that I am one with? Do I *believe* it, maybe because my traditional *faith* tells me I am supposed to? Or do I really *know* it, all the way down to my gut level? How is my current level of awareness serving me and others with whom I interact?

One thing I work on more now than I did then is walking in awareness, and I pray for "Just a closer walk with Thee." I love doing this on hikes and anywhere in nature where God's handiwork is, oh, so evident. I stop to really see and appreciate the infinite ways God expresses as flora and fauna. This feeds my soul, strengthens my connection, and gives me a respite from the constant wheels in motion of my typically busy mind.

I also love moving into situations with the awareness of knowing I may find an opportunity to assist someone. Just yesterday, I went to visit my friend in hospice. It had been a few days since I'd seen him, and he looked like he was not long for this world. I didn't know what else to do, so I just sang the chorus of his favorite song to him, over and over, hoping it would help. I also somehow *knew* to tell him it was okay for him to let go—that God and his loved ones would be waiting for him with open arms on the other side, and that he would feel so much better. He passed peacefully a half hour later.

This is what life can look like when we are loving awareness.

THE VOICE

Annie (Los Angeles, California)

Live each day as if it were your last. This is how to walk in awareness. Never wanting for tomorrow. Only wanting and being grateful for right now. Right here, right now.

Chapter 5, Lesson #3

The third concept in our "Power of Threes" chapter addresses how God expresses Itself in physicality at the most fundamental level:

**THE THREE BASIC PRINCIPLES OF LIFE ARE:
FUNCTIONALITY, ADAPTABILITY, AND SUSTAINABILITY—
REPLACING MORALITY, JUSTICE, AND OWNERSHIP.**

If you happened to catch Neale on *The Today Show* some years ago, you would have heard him say that most of us have gotten our understanding of God "all wrong." He eventually wrote a book about it, titled *God's Message To the World: You've God Me All Wrong*. Throughout history we've fashioned our societies based on false assumptions about what we think God is and what we think It wants. We've caused untold pain and suffering in the process, not just for our own species, but for countless other species with which we share the Earth. We've even caused untold damage to the Earth itself, our physical source of life. No species has been more detrimental to the sustainability of the planet than the human race.

Because of these false assumptions about God, we have created societies with rules based on what we imagine to be right and wrong instead of what works and what doesn't work—morality instead of functionality.

Because of these false assumptions about God, we have created societies where we punish others based on what we imagine they did wrong instead of evolving systems that work for the betterment of all—justice instead of adaptability.

And because of these false assumptions about God, we have created societies where we think it's possible to own things, instead of recognizing our responsibility to simply be good stewards of the things we are given to care for—ownership instead of sustainability.

When Greg and I bought our first house in Orlando, I was surprised to find that our homeowner's insurance wasn't going to cost any more than we had been paying for renter's insurance, even though it covered not only our personal belongings, but also the house itself with all of its appliances and accoutrements. When I asked our insurance agent why, she matter-of-factly replied, "Pride of ownership." She said that as a general rule, people are more inclined to take better care of their home when they own it as opposed to when they rent it.

If we think about this deeply, though, we realize we never really own *anything*. We can call forth a particular thing into our lives and have legal ownership of it, but as the saying goes, "You can't take it with you." If we were a highly evolved society, we would replace "pride of ownership" with "pride of stewardship" and do our best to take good care of the things we're blessed to have in our lives, knowing that we'll be passing them on to someone else someday.

We can take a tip from the founders of the Occupy Chicago movement who adopted the Three Basic Principles of Life from CWG as its foundational bylaws when it created the "Occupy Chicago: Functionality, Adaptability & Sustainability Act." As they grew their grassroots political movement, they were committed to observing what worked for them and to changing what didn't, always with the goal of sustaining their group.

Life is constantly adapting *automatically*. Occupy Chicago and *Conversations with God* point out that as human beings, we can also choose to adapt *consciously*—to consistently work toward changing ourselves for the better. They show us that the way to use today's lesson couldn't be more simple:

Keep doing what works, and change what doesn't.

Please write in your journal or post on the website your answers to the following Self-Reflection Questions:

1. What aspects of your life are working well for you? What must you keep doing to sustain them? What, if anything, must you change in order to sustain them?

2. What aspects of your life are not working for you? Is there a way to change them to make them work better? If not, can you simply let them go?

The following are Action Steps for you to take over the next week:

1. Read or watch the news each day, paying close attention to any stories about political hot-button issues such as abortion, gay marriage, gun control, the death penalty, etc. See if you think the powers that be are attempting to legislate morality—what they believe is right and wrong—or are trying to do what works for the greater good of society. Please write your thoughts about those news stories in your journal or on the website.

2. Read or watch the news each day, paying close attention to any stories about the criminal justice system. See if you can think of a way to resolve

each situation that would work toward bringing about positive change without using punishment. Please write out your ideas.

3. Try to eradicate from your vocabulary the words "my," "mine," "our," "ours," and any other possessive pronouns that signify ownership. See if this changes your thoughts about what you previously declared was "yours," and write about how this makes you feel.

◇◇

Postscript

"How's that workin' for ya?!"

I've heard my fellow CWG Life Coach and Executive Director of the Conversations with God Foundation, JR Westen, ask this question countless times on our Spiritual Mentoring Program group calls. He asks it in a light-hearted way, but always with a serious undertone, and it points to the first Basic Principle of Life: functionality. We must be willing to look candidly at what is functioning and what is *malfunctioning* in our lives if we want to adapt consciously instead of by default. To know what's working and what isn't, we have to know what our intention is in the first place. As *Conversations with God* says, "Life proceeds out of our intention for it."

We use the Three Basic Principles of Life—functionality, adaptability, and sustainability—constantly in all areas of our lives. We just haven't been calling it that. We shape and hone our relationships in order to peacefully co-exist with others. We develop new ideas in the workplace in order for companies to stay in business. And governments are constantly discussing and enacting new laws in order to adapt to ever-changing times.

However, in all areas of our lives, we sometimes get stuck in malfunctioning situations. We stay in relationships with our partners long after the love is gone, even after they become ugly scenarios of emotional or physical abuse. Companies keep their doors open, hoping to turn a profit, even after it's apparent to everyone else that they likely never will. And governments are notorious for wasteful spending on projects that no longer serve us (if they ever did) and on long-lasting wars that undermine the common good.

In order to consciously use the Three Basic Principles of Life to fulfill our intentions, we need to incorporate the Three Core Concepts of Holistic Living: honesty, awareness, and responsibility. We must be willing to ask, then act on, the answer to JR's powerful question: "How's that workin' for ya?!"

THE VOICE

Marie (Queensland, Australia)

For this lesson, in lieu of a quote from *The Voice*, I can think of no better example of how to implement functionality, adaptability, and sustainability than through the post of one of my online students, Marie. Here's how she responded to this lesson's Action Steps:

1. Read or watch the news each day, paying close attention to any stories about political hot-button issues . . . See if you think the powers that be are attempting to legislate morality or are trying to do what works for the greater good of society.

I have been doing this for some time. I have always been conscious of the right and wrong thing and my own feeling of, "Well, who decided this, anyway? God is all-loving." So, for me, very many things don't align with all-loving.

I feel like we live in a world where shame flourishes by making rules about what is right and wrong. I have personal experience of the effects of the rules against gay marriage or that being gay is wrong, as I have watched this impact my son. How he felt like he didn't belong to this world, which eventually became a drug addiction where he escaped it. I cannot imagine a world where we are more inclined to be right than to be kind. Where we are more inclined to shame someone than to love them. Where we decide someone is less than, rather than the same as.

Even in my youth where religion was strongly imposed on me, I used to think, "God would have a reason for all of this. Who am

I to assume that my right and wrong is wiser than God's doing?" I have been blessed to sit in a space of "nothing is right or wrong—it just is" for all of my life. I am grateful for that because it allows me to just love all from the depths of my heart. I believe in the potential of all people, and I believe they are all good (God).

I don't think our society runs at all on the idea of the greater good. I feel like it is competitive, self-justifying, diminishing of others to win, and destructive. I feel sad that the world at large just goes with the flow of systems based on right and wrong and doesn't see that love is the answer.

2. Read or watch the news each day, paying close attention to any stories about the criminal justice system. See if you can think of a way to resolve each situation that would work toward bringing about positive change without using punishment.

I am able to give my own personal account of this as I have just returned from the police station with my son. Here is a beautiful young man that found in his teens he was gay. He went to an all-male Catholic school, and the bullying escalated. He decided there was something wrong with him. He worked hard in the world to overstep this but ended up succumbing to drugs. Now he has been picked up and charged by the police for possession for the third time. When he is arrested he is very obviously high beyond "party high." They find him alone, wandering aimlessly, not connected with reality, thin, and very obviously not okay. So they put him in jail, send him to the courts who fine him, and let him go.

What if we looked beyond right and wrong? What if we asked the question, "Why is this human being so lost?" And what if we recognized that and enforced a recovery program, not one to just stop using, but one to discover why he began? Throwing him to the street with a money fine just makes it worse and drives him further into his deeply destructive life. Is this punishment for him? Not really. His life is already dark. All it is for him is an affirmation that, "I am not a worthy human being." Perhaps it could be a program that helped him find his light again, healed his woundedness, and showed him a world where all people knew they were valid, exactly as they are.

3. Try to eradicate from your vocabulary the words "my," "mine," "our," "ours," and any other possessive pronouns that signify ownership. See if this

changes your thoughts about what you previously declared was "yours," and write about how this makes you feel.

I have begun to do this, and what I have noticed the most is the peace. The pressure is gone of ownership and having to hold on so tightly as to not lose it. I feel relaxed and at peace with the world when I do this, knowing that I can just appreciate everything in my world, care for it, and love it.

Chapter 5, Lesson #4

The final concept in our "Power of Threes" chapter further develops one of our earlier ones: "You are the creator of your own reality." It packs the most personal power punch of any of *Conversations with God*'s 25 Core Concepts, and it's aptly titled:

The Three Declarations of Empowerment from the Triad Process are:

NOTHING IN MY WORLD IS REAL;

THE MEANING OF EVERYTHING IS THE MEANING I GIVE IT;

I AM WHO I SAY I AM, AND MY EXPERIENCE IS WHAT I SAY IT IS.

Neale says that one of the most non-beneficial questions we can ask ourselves when going through a very difficult situation is, "Why?"

It's, of course, perfectly natural to wonder, "Why is this happening to me?" when we're trying to make sense of a challenge, but it can completely derail our joy and peace when we can't answer it. As I've heard him point out many times, we can assign meaning to an event at any time, and later, when we have a broader perspective, we can almost always come up with at least one very good reason why something unpleasant happened. Sometimes it may have been more for someone else's benefit than our own.

But in the right here, right now moment of, "This is really hard, and I don't like it," sometimes all we can do is trust the process, knowing that everything happens for our growth and greater good; knowing that we are part of God, and God doesn't make mistakes; knowing that this experience contains a gift for us, as has everything else we've gone through, when enough time has passed for us to see what it is.

It's also helpful when going through a challenging time, to remember that all experiences here are temporary, and this illusory realm is not as real as it may seem. Remember how the Toltecs and others believe that "life is but a dream"?

If you believed this were true, could you relax into life more and allow others to live their dream the way they choose? Could you accept the troubles of the world a bit better? Could you allow yourself to be completely joyful in spite of them and in spite of anything in your own dream that seems out of place? Could you nip your negative thoughts in the bud as soon as they pop up, realizing, "Oh, that isn't really true; I'm just making that up"? Could you do this for just one day?!

Guess what, folks? You *can* do this. I know because *I* can, and on more and more days lately, I do it all day long. I wake up with a smile on my face, thanking God for this beautiful day and this beautiful life with all of its blessings, and I keep wearing that smile all day long. I end my day with the same heartfelt prayers of gratitude before falling asleep. And the more I feel this good and grateful, the more life gives me to feel good and grateful about. As my friend Gaia said to me, "It just gets better and better!"

Please write in your journal or post on the website your answers to the following Self-Reflection Questions:

1. Has there been a difficult event or circumstance in your life that you feel you have yet to come to terms with? Can you assign meaning to it now? Realizing you don't know why it happened, ask yourself this ubiquitous question of Neale's: "I *know* you don't know, but if you *thought* you knew, what would your answer be?" Please write about that process.

2. What are the three most difficult things you remember going through, and what meaning or meanings have you assigned to each of them? Again, if you don't know why it happened, just *make up* a reason.

The following are Action Steps for you to take over the next week:

1. If you read or watch the news regularly, allow yourself to take a break from it. If something really important happens, rest assured you'll hear about

it. In the time you usually spend paying attention to the news, spend it instead in meditation, pondering this lesson's concept.

2. Read the book *Illusions: The Adventures of a Reluctant Messiah* by Richard Bach. It's a quick read, but full of little wisdoms, and it may help you understand today's concept a bit more fully. Feel free to post any thoughts or questions about the book on the website.

Postscript

One of my favorite ministers, Rev. Larry Schellink of Unity of Santa Barbara, said something recently that sent me diving into my purse for a pen:

A SETBACK IS JUST A SETUP FOR A COMEBACK.

I liked the quote and his talk so much, I got a copy of it on CD and have listened to it several times. I later learned that the quote is credited to a Baptist minister and civil rights leader, Dr. Benjamin Mays. Dating back to 1983, this quote can now be found on motivational plaques, signs, and posters. There's even a book by that title. This doesn't surprise me because sometimes the most insightful truths are found in the fewest words. This gives us plenty of room to mull them over and digest their implications for ourselves.

This succinct sentence, "A setback is just a setup for a comeback," builds on the traditional Christian adage, "Don't judge by appearances." It actually goes one step further, suggesting that if we approach the situation with the right attitude, what's happening may not be as bad as it seems and can even become the catalyst for something greater.

Neale's book, *When Everything Changes, Change Everything*, expounds this idea in innovative ways. As he was writing it, he told Greg and me what it was about and invited us to compose a song for it, which he later included on CD in a limited edition signed and numbered series of the book. This song, more than any other that Greg and I have co-written, took the longest because we kept *changing* it! I remember countless times I would get out of bed in the middle of the night to write down just one more little tweak . . . It took three months to finish the song and get into the studio to record it. Think about it: What Neale had three hundred pages to say, we had to get down in a three minute song. No wonder I obsessed about it! I think what we eventually ended up with, though, got the point across pretty well. Here are the lyrics to "Change Everything" in their final form as heard on the recording:

Stop the world, it's moving far too fast
The future I see looks nothing like the past
Did I build my house just to watch it fall?
Did I save for rainy days just to lose it all?

What we do, what we say
How we think and how we pray
What seems right and what seems wrong

What we've longed for, for so long
When everything changes, change everything

I felt left out, so I dove right in
Changed my mind, then took a look again
I saw a shift right before my eyes
A loss can be a gift, now I realize

What we do, what we say
How we think and how we pray
What seems right and what seems wrong
What we've longed for, for so long
When everything changes, change everything

I'm not a ship that's tossed about, a boat without an oar
My pebble dropped into a pond makes waves on every shore

What we do, what we say
How we think and how we pray
What seems right and what seems wrong
What we've lived for, for so long
When everything changes, when everything changes
When everything changes, change everything

THE VOICE

Sophie (Boulogne, France)

Q: Dear God, I would like to understand what "Nothing in my world is real" means.

Dear child, everything around you is but an illusion—one you have created as a race, to enjoy life on Earth—and can change at any given moment. What's real is love; the energy that sustains it; the energy that gives life. So the way you use the planet's resources and treat the animals and each other—yourselves—can derive from love/life or from fear/death. Since death is also an illusion bringing you back to life, you're just going in circles until you choose love consciously, thus enjoying life.

You can go further and understand that more is invisible than visible. What your senses perceive is but the tip of the iceberg. What really matters is invisible. For example, you can't see or touch love. Still, as I have just taught you, nothing else is real. When you become aware of this truth, you may want to start acting from the heart instead of the mind.

Let's say someone you hold dear is taking some distance from you. If you look at it from your mind or from a visible/logical angle, you may start

judging the situation as unbearable or unfair. You may wonder what you did
wrong or decide you are being wronged. If you look at it from your heart—
with your soul's eyes—you will open yourself to a world of possibilities, none
of which relate to blame, judgment, or fear. Compassion for yourself and for
that person shall guide you. You may choose to go; you may choose to wait
and see. But whatever you do, you'll respect yourself and the other involved.

Q: I see. That brings me to my second question. Can I really give the meaning I want to any given occurrence in my life or in the world?

Sure you can. There is a difference between blaming others or circumstances
and giving something a meaning. If you choose to hold others responsible for
what is happening to you, you are actually ripping it of any meaning. There
could be many meanings. Choose the one that brings you peace.

Q: Lastly, I am very moved by the concept, "I am who I say I am, and my
experience is what I say it is." To be honest, though, I wonder if it isn't a
great pitfall for my ego.

It all depends on your intention and who leads the way in your life: your heart, your mind, or your soul? A harmonious combination of the three?

Let me give you an example: Say you declare, "I am right all the time, and my experience is that I am here to teach what is right." Would it ring true to your soul?

No, but my ego has had many field days with that one!

How did it go?

Badly and sadly. It never led anywhere pleasant or productive.

So what would your soul choose to declare on that matter? How would she word it?

I am a teacher, and my experience is that I enjoy passing along messages and experiences that have helped me grow, so as to help others grow as well.

Hmmmmm . . . Quite different.

Yes, I realize that. But what about grief? How do you change that experience?

You trust in each other's love. In My love. In the fact that no thing is a punishment of any kind but really is what you decide to label it. Let's say a child—an infant—dies. How would you label it?

Unfair; terrible; unbearably sad.

That is your gut response as a mother and is humanely understandable and logical. Now, how would your soul label it?

Karmic. To be respected and accepted—even if not understood—as an opportunity to grow in compassion and to nurture the grieving parents.

One event; two visions. Who were you in the first instance?

A judge.

And in the second one?

A child of God; a fellow human.

So who are you, and what is your experience in this life?

I am a child of God, and my experience is that life is magically beautiful and beautifully magic. Thank you.

WHO YOU ARE & MOVING BEYOND THE ILLUSIONS

Chapter 6, Lesson #1

Our final chapter is titled "Who You Are & Moving Beyond the Illusions." Until we realize who we really are—individuated aspects of God—and until we see the Physical Realm for what it is—an illusion—we won't move beyond ordinary experience. There are people like you and me who have walked this Earth and done what we would call miraculous things, and there still are—people whose level of awareness is the highest: the level of knowing who they really are and knowing they have the power to control the illusion. They can then use that powerful knowledge to do amazing things.

One of the world's largest religions is based on one such man. Yet if Jesus the Christ were alive today, I think he would joyfully acknowledge that he wasn't the only one with this power. He told his followers they would do such works as he did, and even greater. He also said, "I and the Father are One." Jesus knew his power came from unity with God, and he was the embodiment of what I hope all of you will embrace fully as a result of this final chapter:

1. To know who you really are, and begin to really *use* that power of God in you, *as* you, to create your experience in the next grandest version of the greatest vision you ever held about yourself.

2. To see this illusory Physical Realm for what it really is—a collectively created, continually changing hologram in which things are not nearly what they seem. Laws of physics as we currently understand them go flying out the window when one reaches mastery.

Over the next four weeks we'll take a good look at how we've made it up in our minds so far, and how we can make it up from here on out. We'll begin with an exploration of the glorious gift that God has given us in dividing Itself so we can express as our wonderful, unique selves:

YOU ARE NOT YOUR BODY, YOU ARE NOT YOUR MIND,
YOU ARE NOT YOUR SOUL;
IT IS THE UNIQUE COMBINATION OF ALL THREE
WHICH COMPRISES THE TOTALITY OF YOU.

This is true not only here in the Realm of the Physical, but also in the Realm of the Spiritual. It may come as a bit of a surprise that *Conversations with God* says we actually retain our body when we die, but anyone who has ever seen a ghost knows this already. Each of us has an ethereal body that goes on, and it is easily recognizable by those who have known us.

We also retain our mind, as many people who have been pronounced dead and come back will tell you. The thinking process never stops as we move forward, demonstrating that thoughts come from the mind, not the brain.

Our soul is that part of us that is constantly tuned into the one big soul—God—so it obviously goes on. Many people think that *only* the soul continues the journey once we cross over, but it is the totality of who we are that makes the continuing eternal journey from the Realm of the Physical, through the Realm of Pure Being, to the Realm of the Spiritual, then back through the Realm of Pure Being, to the Realm of the Physical, and so on and so on. Picture a figure 8 on its side. The Realm of the Physical/Relative is one circle, the Realm of the Spiritual/Absolute is the other circle, and the Realm of Pure Being is the point in the middle where the two circles meet. The Realm of Pure Being is the doorway between the two other realms, where we transition from one "side" to the other.

Our body, mind, and soul together make the journey, yet it is the soul that has the ultimate say-so when it's time to move to another realm. As CWG says, the body and mind sometimes will not be ready to move on, so the soul may go along with them and delay the transition for awhile, but ultimately when the soul is done, it is done, and off we go! We often place great negative judgment on transitions from the Physical to the Spiritual, calling an "untimely death" a tragedy, but to the soul, everything is perfect and joyous. Most of us simply don't have enough information about how life works to get out of our judgment that death is a bad thing. According to CWG and to the people who remember having "died" and come back, when we cross over to the Spiritual Realm and reacquaint ourselves with the Light of Love, we experience greater joy than we have ever known here on Earth!

So how can we use all three aspects of our being to create a better life while here in the Physical Realm?

First, take good care of all three parts of you. Here are some suggestions:

1. Nurture your body with plenty of rest, clean water and air, and healthy, whole organic foods. Do weight-bearing exercise, aerobic exercise (a nice brisk walk is enough), and stretching (simple yoga moves are very therapeutic). Treat yourself to a massage now and then.

2. Nurture your mind by keeping it sharp. Do crossword puzzles, play solitaire or Scrabble, or anything that requires your mind to recall and organize data. Read high quality and sometimes mentally challenging material in lieu of junk novels. Most importantly, pay attention to what you're thinking about. Don't camp out in fear, unresolved anger, or anxiety, and don't wallow in worry or blame about yourself or anyone else. (Metaphysically speaking, we do someone a disservice when we worry about them.) Keep your mind focused on love as the greatest power in your life.

3. Nurture your soul by setting aside quiet reflective time. Go within in meditation or prayer, and take walks in nature to see for yourself the great goodness of God in Its infinite forms. Be careful what you feed your soul. Don't watch too much bad news or violence as they can zap your joy in an instant. Find a spiritual center or group of like-minded people, or start one so you will have continuing support on your spiritual journey. Offer your knowledge of CWG concepts to others who may benefit from your larger

understandings. In helping others, you help yourself, and this feeds your soul in the most wonderful way.

The second way to make this concept useful is to be aware of *why* you are a three-part being, and then to use that information accordingly. The Three Functions of Life according to *Conversations with God* are:

1. The function of the soul is to indicate its desires (not impose them).

2. The function of the mind is to choose from its alternatives.

3. The function of the body is to act out that choice.

Use your mind to create the *experience* of your body and soul by always rising to your highest thought about *everything*.

The soul has a broader perspective and, therefore, the highest knowing. The mind has a very limited perspective, so will often try to fill in the gaps of what it doesn't know. The good news is, we get to choose the way we think, and the soul will always guide us if we just pay attention. It's easy, really, with these benchmarks: When we feel good, we are thinking rightly and are in alignment with our soul's highest knowing. When we don't feel good, we aren't, and it's time to examine those thoughts. This excerpt from the "Affirmation for Life" bears repeating:

How I choose to think creates my personal experience.

Please write in your journal or post on the website your answers to the following Self-Reflection Questions:

1. Do you think it is possible to die at an inappropriate time? If so, according to whose ideas of what is inappropriate? Yours or someone else's?

2. Do you feel joyful about the idea, "I get to keep coming back over and over again!" or do you perhaps feel somewhat despondent or even depressed by the idea? If it doesn't sound joyful to you because life has been hard, please know that nothing is forced upon you. *You* get to decide if, when, and how to come back. CWG's Third Statement of Ultimate Truth, "There is nothing you have to do," applies to both the Physical and Spiritual Realms. You are always at choice in the matter.

3. Please write your thoughts and feelings about your eternal journey in your journal or on the website.

The following are Action Steps for you to take over the next week:

1. Watch the documentary *Life After Life* on YouTube or Amazon Prime's Gaia channel. Based on the best-selling book by Dr. Raymond A. Moody, Jr., and produced and directed by our friend, Peter Shockey, the film shows numerous firsthand accounts of people who have been pronounced clinically dead, then come to back to tell about it. After watching this powerful

film, if you previously had fear around death and dying, you likely won't have it anymore.

2. Add the book *Eight Weeks to Optimum Health* by Dr. Andrew Weil to your library, and begin implementing its positive changes into your lifestyle.

3. If you haven't read *When Everything Changes, Change Everything*, please begin reading it now. If you have already read it, please review the WECCE Model's Mechanics of the Mind and System of the Soul. Try to grasp the model's full meaning, and if you have any questions about it, please post them for me on the website or on WECCE's free website, www.cwghelpingoutreach.com. There are many volunteer Spiritual Helpers there who would relish the opportunity to be of assistance to you.

Postscript

Do you know that the Totality of You was overjoyed when it chose to come into this physical incarnation? Your ethereal body, mind, and soul were thrilled at the infinite opportunities that being born into this existence held for you. Yet how many people do we see every day who look miserable?

After Neale's retreats when I'm floating through the airport on cloud nine, I'm always struck by how many people are rushing to and fro with knitted eyebrows, eyes cast low, and by all appearances, hating life. How can this be, in our modern-day society where we've been given so many conveniences designed to make life easier? In these times in which we can simply hand someone a little card, then walk onto a jet and fly anywhere in the world we want?

Does anyone realize what a gift this is? Does anyone besides me see what an awesome gift life on this beautiful planet Earth is?! And if you're one of those people who are miserable or maybe just feeling lackadaisical about life, how did you get that way? Could it be from from spending too much time in your mind at the expense of your soul?

Neale's book, *The Only Thing That Matters*, tells us how we can integrate all three parts of ourselves—body, mind, and soul—in our day-to-day experience. It says our souls most assuredly had agendas in coming here. Do you know what yours is? If you know it, do you spend the majority of your time doing it? Do you spend any time at *all* doing it? It appears that some people don't, and that's why they feel unfulfilled.

It seems that many of us either don't know, don't believe, or don't act on the message given to us in Chapter 1, Lesson #3: "There is nothing you have to do." We allow everything our mind thinks we *should* do to take precedence over everything our soul would *love* to do. Sure, we all have responsibilities in life, especially if we have children, and we want to keep a roof over their heads and food in their bellies. The irony is, though, sometimes the very thing our soul wants to do would be the greatest provider for all of that.

PROSPERITY GROWS WHERE PASSION FLOWS.

This is because when we're excited by something our soul would love to do, and we allow our mind and body to follow its indication, we feel happy and fulfilled. Joy is our natural vibratory state, and it is magnetic, drawing the perfect people and situations to us, which allows us to continue what we're so happily doing. We are in a state of non-resistance, so all the good of the Universe flows unimpeded to us. Sure, life will offer up some bumps in the road now and then. It always does. But when we're living from our natural states of being, we sail pretty smoothly through them.

Choosing to stay focused on our connection to God during the rough times alleviates the suffering. We feel the pain of the experience but choose not to suffer, knowing that everything is happening perfectly even when our former selves who didn't know better wouldn't have thought so. Getting back to our joy of coming into physicality comes down to dropping our judgment.

This doesn't mean dropping our discernment. We all need to look at our responsibilities in life and decide which ones are most important to us. Every single thing we are doing now began as a conscious decision to do it. Yet if we find we are no longer enjoying whatever we're doing, we get to choose again! If we want to lead a happy life, we must strike a balance between things we do for maintenance of the body and things we do for joy of the soul. Remember, the mind's job is to choose from the alternatives.

I have a dear friend who says her favorite thing in the world is to paint. She is very talented, and everyone loves her paintings—when she takes the time to do them, which usually isn't very often. I think she feels she doesn't have time to paint because she has to spend most of her time trying to make money to pay the bills. It's almost as if her life has to look a certain way before she will focus on the "luxury" of doing what she loves most. Although I've suggested to her that prosperity follows passion, and she can sell her artwork, and even though her own CWGs have told her to *just paint*, she still rarely finds time to do it. This is so typical of the human experience; who can blame her? Yet this is what I have come to believe about that:

WE DON'T *FIND* TIME TO DO WHAT WE LOVE;
WE *MAKE* TIME TO DO WHAT WE LOVE.

It's up to each of us to choose how to bring joy to all the moments of our lives. Whether to follow our soul's indicators or not is a choice we all get to make because the soul's function is to indicate its desires, not impose them. I believe we could reclaim the great thrill we had in coming to the Earth if we would strike a balance between body, mind, and soul. At least it's a good place to start . . .

THE VOICE

PJ (Las Vegas, Nevada)

The balanced combination of your mind, body, and soul is what makes you whole, complete, and unique. Love is the language of the soul, and it connects us to our Self and to All. Choking off any part of who we are leaves us imbalanced, incomplete, out of integrity, and feeling disconnected. Being in integrity empowers us to be our Highest Self.

Chapter 6, Lesson #2

NEED, FAILURE, DISUNITY, INSUFFICIENCY, REQUIREMENT, JUDGMENT, CONDEMNATION, CONDITIONALITY, SUPERIORITY, AND IGNORANCE DO NOT EXIST.
THESE ARE THE TEN ILLUSIONS OF HUMANS.

There's an adage that modern-day sports teams have borrowed from the Dalai Lama that says, "When you lose, don't lose the lesson." Although I don't participate in competitive sports, I like the idea that something valuable can be gained even if we fall short of a goal. It's 4:00 am, and I just woke up and realized what the lesson was in something I did that fell way short of who I know I am. Here's what happened:

One of my online students, Uma, and I made an agreement with each other to commit a "random act of kindness" every day for a month. We've been emailing each other back and forth to share our experiences and to help hold each other accountable. Last night, I felt compelled to confess to Greg that I had committed a random act of *unkindness* and felt terrible about it.

I was running late for a doctor's appointment yesterday, and the parking garage was fuller than I had ever seen it. I drove around and around several times looking for a parking space, then as I turned a corner, I spied one and quickly went for it. Just before pulling in, I saw there was a car across from me with its blinker on, indicating it was waiting for that space. Normally I would move on and look for another, but I was still in hurry-up mode and had already committed in my mind to turning, so I whipped into the space, disregarding the other driver. Immediately my *Voice* let me know this was definitely not my highest choice, but I had reacted so quickly I didn't know what to do except get out of the car and hope that she had gone. Well, this gal wasn't going anywhere until she let me know that I had acted rudely, and she said, "My indicator light was on for that spot." I was so flustered, I lied and told her I hadn't noticed. How childish is that?! As I frantically tried to think of a way to rectify the situation, I spied a free space right around the corner that she couldn't see, so I offered to move my car there and give her the spot I was in. She said, "No problem," and drove on to the other spot. I was left with nothing to do but hurry in to my appointment and feel lousy while the doctor kept me waiting for the better part of an hour. Duh.

Conversations with God talks about the difference between creating our experiences rather than reacting to them. It cleverly points out that it's all about how we see things, or "c" them, because the main difference in the words "create" and "react" is where the "c" is. My reaction showed that I wasn't seeing clearly, and as a result, I didn't create that scenario in my highest way. Far from it. But later in the day, I read about someone so highly evolved, he created an incredible response to an extreme experience.

I was reading *Autobiography of a Yogi* which is full of examples of miraculous things that Indian masters have done, including this one:

> Two policemen were looking for a murderer who was disguised as a holy man. They thought they had found the suspect, and approaching him from behind, ordered him to stop. The man disregarded them and kept walking, so one of the policemen wielded his ax hard and nearly severed his

arm! Turns out, he really *was* a holy man, not the murderer, and he had no outward reaction at all. He kept right on walking without even glancing down at his dangling arm, so the policemen ran in front of him to talk with him. The holy man said, "I am not the murderer you are seeking. Son, that was just an understandable mistake on your part. Run along, and don't reproach yourself. The Beloved Mother is taking care of me." And with that, he popped his arm back into place, and the bleeding stopped. He said further, "Come to me under yonder tree in three days, and you will find me fully healed. Thus, you will feel no remorse." Sure enough, in three days, his arm had completely healed, and there wasn't even a hint of a scar.

So here I am in the wee hours of the morning, comparing our reactions. I see that I have a long way to go in really getting the basic principles of this teaching. What did my reaction in the parking lot illustrate? That at a fundamental reactionary level, all my training flew out the window. For a brief moment I obviously believed in need (I thought I needed that parking space), failure (I thought I might fail to get a space), disunity (I forgot the gal in that car and I are one), insufficiency (I didn't think there were enough empty parking spots even though there was one just out of sight), requirement (I incorrectly thought I was required to be on time), superiority (I got here first, dammit!) and ignorance (I didn't know any better than to pull a stupid stunt like that). Whew, that's a whopping seven illusions. Add my later judgment and condemnation of my actions, and we're up to nine out of the Ten Illusions of Humans. Not so good, to say the least.

But even though I lost my sense of who I am for a few moments, the lesson I gained from the experience is this: We will know we have fully embraced the *Conversations with God* teaching when our reactions that illustrate it are *automatic*. When we don't just get it *some* of the time, but when we get it *all* of the time, and our actions prove it. When every action and *reaction* is a holy creation.

◇◇◇

Please write in your journal or post on the website your answers to the following Self-Reflection Questions:

Are you able to live your life as a constant example of your highest knowing of who you are, or do you sometimes fall back into coming from some of the Ten Illusions in your thoughts, words, or actions? If not, what percentage of the time are you able to do so? What would it take to increase that? Please elaborate.

The following are Action Steps for you to take over the next week:

1. Say this prayer every morning before you get out of bed: "Thank you, God, for another day, full of opportunities for me to be my highest and best." Make this a regular spiritual practice, so when life suddenly throws you a curve, you'll be ready to automatically respond from your highest knowing instead of your old paradigms.

2. Set an intention to do a "random act of kindness" every day. See how this makes you feel, and write about those experiences in your journal or on the website.

3. Read *Communion with God* for an in-depth explanation of this lesson's concept. If you've already read it, please read it again.

Postscript

I recently experienced a series of events that gave me the perfect opportunity to remember the Ten Illusions and to happily create my experience by not buying into them. It was a very interesting couple of days. Here's what happened:

I was scheduled to fly from Los Angeles to Dallas at 11:20 am on a Friday. I was excited to go celebrate my niece's high school graduation and my sister's (her mom's) birthday, and to see their new house. As Greg and I neared the airport, I checked my email on my phone and saw an alert from American Airlines that said my flight was delayed until 2:00 pm. Uh-oh. This would cause some problems for my sister, as I would land a half hour late for our 6:30 dinner reservation, not counting the long travel time from the airport. I thought to myself, "Well, I may have to Uber, and that's gonna be expensive, but it is what it is. We'll figure it out, one way or another."

So I said to Greg, "Let's go out to breakfast since there's no hurry to get me to the airport." We found a restaurant and had just ordered when I checked my phone again. Another email had come in that said, "Your flight is now departing on time at 11:20."

Omigosh! We quickly cancelled our order and rushed to the airport, as I was now later than I normally like to arrive at LAX before a flight.

Email updates kept coming in that were very unusual, such as, "Your departure gate is now the Tom Bradley International Terminal." Really? To Dallas?! Okay . . . I was in hurry-up mode by this time and running to try to find the gate. Only when I got to security did I realize I'd forgotten to check my bag. I have never done this in all the many flights I've taken over the years. I remembered, though, that I've seen agents take oversized bags at the gate, so I figured, "Well, I'll just have to do that." When I found my gate, though, there was no one there. There were no staff or passengers and no signage indicating a flight to Dallas. I waited a few minutes for someone to show up. When no one did, I checked my phone again, and lo and behold, found another email saying we'd had a gate change back to Terminal 4. *Omigosh!* How in the world was I ever going to get there in time? I would have to leave the building, walk to the other terminal, then go through security again—or so I thought. I didn't even know my way out of where I was. I started running at a full sprint this time, pulling my bag behind me, and found some "exit" signs. I was about to follow them when a security agent stopped me and asked where I was going. I told him, and he said, "You don't want to go that way, or you'll have to go through security all over again. Here's a hallway that will take you right to the secured area of Terminal 4." I could have kissed him!

I made it to the new gate and told the agent I'd forgotten to check my bag, so she tagged it for me. Now there was nothing to do but sit back, catch my breath, and wait to board. A few minutes later she announced we would be delayed by ten minutes, so they were changing our gate. This time it was no big deal as the other gate was right next to where we were, and a ten minute delay didn't matter. A little later she said, "We'll be boarding in five minutes." "Yay!" I thought. "I'll make it to the airport in Dallas in plenty of time and won't mess up my sister's dinner plans. Perfect!" Within minutes, however, I glanced up at the sign, and in bright yellow letters it said, "Now leaving 7:00 pm." "What?!!!" I exclaimed, louder than I meant to. "Seven o'clock?!" That wouldn't put us in Dallas until midnight.

This is the point where, I'm pleased to say, I was able to use my understanding of the Ten Illusions to create peace around the situation. This "last straw" gave me an inner knowing that I wasn't supposed to be on this flight, so I got in line to cancel it and get my bag back. I had neither a *need* to go as it was just a pleasure trip, nor a *requirement* that it be "my way or the highway." I didn't allow the trip to Dallas to be a *condition* necessary for my happiness. I didn't *judge* it as a bad thing or *condemn* the situation. Instead of *ignorance* about the situation, I knew it must be for my highest and best, or it wouldn't be happening. I stayed grounded in my non-belief in *disunity* as I interacted with the customer service rep. I came from Oneness, and was as kind to her as possible, knowing that none of this was her fault. I think she must have appreciated it because she not only gave me a full refund, she also gave me 12,000 bonus miles for my trouble!

Because my bag was right there at the gate, I was able to waltz out of the airport with nary a care. Maybe that part was Divine Intervention because, if I had remembered to check my bag as usual, and the airline had taken it into their system, it certainly would have been no small effort to retrieve it.

By surrendering to the circumstances and allowing the event to unfold in its own way, I saved myself a lot of grief. After Greg came back to the airport to pick me up, American changed the departure *five more times* to 8:00 pm, 9:00 pm, 5:00 am the next day, 8:00 am, then 9:03 am. Wow.

This episode made it clearer than ever that I can't control conditions, but I *can* control my attitude, and attitude is everything. As my friend Gregory says, "It's insane to try to push the river. The river remains completely nonplussed and we just end up getting all wet." I know I am way happier when I choose to go with the flow. Here are some ways to do that, by using the Ten Illusions:

1. Stop needing things to show up a certain way in order for you to be happy. (no need)

2. Know that you cannot fail, as God always has your back, and life is always conspiring in your favor. (no failure)

3. See God in everyone and everything around you, and allow yourself to feel your natural love that radiates from that knowing. (no disunity)

4. Notice that you have enough of everything you need, right here, right now. How can you know this? Because you are *still here*, on the planet, living and breathing. (no insufficiency)

5. Stop putting requirements on yourself and others to show up a certain way. (no requirement)

6. Stop judging things that seem to be bad. They wouldn't be happening the way they are if it weren't for the highest good. (no judgment)

7. Stop condemning yourself and others for what you perceive to be short-comings. (no condemnation)

8. Work toward unconditional love for yourself and others. We are all individuations of God, and for that fact alone, are worthy of love and compassion. (no conditionality)

9. Remember that no one is better than anyone else. We're all in this together, whether we realize it or not. (no superiority)

10. Know that you know everything you need to know in order to make it in this world. If there is confusion in your mind, go within to gain clarity from your soul. It's the larger part of you that sees all, knows all, and loves all. (no ignorance)

THE VOICE

Cynthia (Atlanta, Georgia)

I am not like your father or mother on Earth, or any religion. They learned like everyone else to put conditions on love. That was part of their survival. Yet I tell you that I don't need anything in return from you to love you. I just love you. I am your father, your mother, your child, your friend, your brother, and your sister. I am everything and everyone that you see and everything that you feel.

Q: I understand that, but how can I trust that you don't want to hurt me?

You don't have to trust in anything at all. You can just look around you and ask yourself, "Is what I am fearing true? Is God really that mean? Do I think that God wants to punish me because this is what I do to others when they make mistakes or when they hurt me? Such as, I become resentful and distant?"

If your answer to this is "yes," then this is why you see Me as someone who punishes, but you think I am in your image instead of seeing it the other way around.

Chapter 6, Lesson #3

We're going to do something a little different with today's concept, as it is the longest, and is really a two-part concept: Five Fallacies About God and Five Fallacies About Life. We'll break the concept down into its two parts, then tie them back together at the end of the lesson.

The Following Statements are Fallacies About God:

1. GOD NEEDS SOMETHING.

2. GOD CAN FAIL TO GET WHAT GOD NEEDS.

3. GOD HAS SEPARATED YOU FROM GOD BECAUSE YOU HAVE NOT GIVEN GOD WHAT GOD NEEDS.

4. GOD STILL NEEDS WHAT GOD NEEDS SO BADLY THAT GOD NOW REQUIRES YOU, FROM YOUR SEPARATED POSITION, TO PROVIDE IT.

5. GOD WILL DESTROY YOU IF YOU DO NOT MEET GOD'S REQUIREMENTS.

Many of us were taught these statements as children, but even then they didn't make sense to me. Fortunately, the Episcopal church where I grew up focused on the love of God much more than on dogmatic statements such as these. However, many churches made them the overriding messages, and still do today.

If we look at each of these statements in relation to the foundational religious tenets on which they are based, we can quickly see that they don't hold water. For example:

1. *God needs something.* If God is Omnipresent and Omniscient, as virtually all religious texts assert, how can It need anything? If we can agree that

God *is* Everything, Everywhere and God *knows* Everything, Everywhere, It either has everything it could possibly need, or It knows how to create it.

2. *God can fail to get what God needs.* If God is Omnipotent, as virtually all religious texts assert, how can It fail to get anything? If we can agree that God *is* All-Powerful, then It cannot fail at anything, including getting a perceived need.

3. *God has separated you from God because you have not given God what God needs.* If God is Omnipresent—Everything, Everywhere—how can It ever be separate from the parts of Itself?

4. *God still needs what god needs so badly that God now requires you, from your separated position, to provide it.* If God is Omnipotent—All-Powerful—then It has the power to provide Its own needs if It, indeed, has any.

5. *God will destroy you if you do not meet God's requirements.* If God is Omnipresent—Everything, Everywhere—why would It destroy a part of Itself?

Let's see how these statements align with the concept we studied in our previous lesson, the Ten Illusions of Humans from *Communion with God:*

1. *God needs something.* Illusion #1: Need exists.

2. *God can fail to get what God needs.* Illusions #2 and #1: Failure exists and Need exists.

3. *God has separated you from God because you have not given God what God needs.* Illusions #3 and #1: Disunity exists and Need exists.

4. *God still needs what God needs so badly that God now requires you, from your separated position, to provide it.* Illusions #1 and #5: Need exists and Requirement exists.

5. *God will destroy you if you do not meet God's requirements.* Illusions #7 and #5: Condemnation exists and Requirement exists. Illusions #6 and #8 are also implied: Judgment exists and Conditionality exists.

Let's move on to the second part of today's concept and see how *these* statements align with the Ten Illusions:

The Following Statements are Fallacies About Life:

1. HUMAN BEINGS ARE SEPARATE FROM EACH OTHER.

2. THERE IS NOT ENOUGH OF WHAT HUMAN BEINGS NEED TO BE HAPPY.

3. TO GET THE STUFF OF WHICH THERE IS NOT ENOUGH HUMAN BEINGS MUST COMPETE WITH EACH OTHER.

4. SOME HUMAN BEINGS ARE BETTER THAN OTHER HUMAN BEINGS.

5. IT IS APPROPRIATE FOR HUMAN BEINGS TO RESOLVE SEVERE DIFFERENCES CREATED BY ALL THE OTHER FALLACIES BY KILLING EACH OTHER.

1. *Human beings are separate from each other.* Illusion #3: Disunity exists.

2. *There is not enough of what human beings need to be happy.* Illusions #4 and #1: Insufficiency exists and Need exists.

3. *To get the stuff of which there is not enough human beings must compete with each other.* Illusion #4: Insufficiency exists.

4. *Some human beings are better than other human beings.* Illusion #9: Superiority exists.

5. *It is appropriate for human beings to resolve severe differences created by all the other fallacies by killing each other.* Illusions #3, #6, #7 and #9: Disunity exists, Judgment exists, Condemnation exists, and Superiority exists.

And in all of the above fallacies about God and life, one Illusion aligns with them all: Illusion #10: Ignorance exists. Many of us think we don't know that these are fallacious statements that people just made up, when in fact, our Higher Selves most certainly know better.

Remember, when we know better, we *do* better, and that is how we make today's extraordinary concept useful. As we come from our highest knowing in our choices and actions, we show up for life the best way we know how. Then others begin to take notice, and we lead by example. No preaching, no dogma, no fallacies about God and life; just shifting the energy naturally, by living at a higher vibration. Remember this:

Higher Vibes = Positive Shift

And folks, shift happens! One person at a time . . .

◇◇◇

Please write in your journal or post on the website your answer to the following Self-Reflection Question:

List three times that you rose to your highest knowing in response to an action that might normally have pulled you off balance. In each instance, describe your thought process about it and what happened as a result.

How do you feel about the way you handled these situations and what, if anything, did you gain from them?

The following are Action Steps for you to take over the next week:

1. Please examine the following major areas of your life to see if there is anything going on right now that it might serve you to rise to a higher vibration about:

Occupation

Health

Relationships

Finances

In each area, look to see if you are living your highest knowing about it, and if you feel you are not, ask God for guidance. Then go within, and allow that guidance to come. Don't disregard the messages you get from your Higher Self as folly! Trust your instincts, and do what feels good and right.

2. Read *The New Revelations*. If you've read it already, please read it again.

◇◇

Postscript

I recently started a Conversations with God Spiritual Study Group in Los Angeles. Although there are dozens of these groups around the world, surprisingly, there wasn't one in LA, so I took the initiative to get one going. In order to find people who might be interested, I posted an announcement online. A week and a half ago, I received this message from a woman named Susan:

Hi Annie,

May I ask you a question? Is Neale a Christian?

Thank you.

Boy, talk about a loaded question. I decided to keep my reply short and simple:

> Hi Susan,
>
> Sorry, but I can't deem to speak for Neale. Christianity is such a broad term, too, with so many different denominations. I do personally feel that *Conversations with God* and Jesus' teachings are not at odds. Hope this helps.

Her response:

> Thanks, Annie,
>
> I was asking entirely outside of religious denomination. I wondered if Neale had accepted Christ as his Lord and Savior. Too many people out there are trying to capture all audiences and referring to "the Universe" and other such terms for God.
>
> Jesus said, "I am the way and the truth and the light. No one comes to the Father except by me." I am seeking teachers who believe that.
>
> Sincerely,
>
> Susan :)

I suppose she added the smiley face at the end to try to keep the conversation light-hearted because it's such a weighty topic. My inclination was to leave it at that, so I did. That is, until yesterday when, for some reason, I picked it back up again. In hindsight, I think I know why. A few days ago, I had a good long catch-up call with one of my closest friends in Nashville, Joanne. She was telling me about a co-worker who she really likes who calls her "the crazy little California liberal." He calls her that because she is very vocal regarding her nonbelief in the Five Fallacies about God, although she doesn't call it that. Being raised in San Francisco, as far as you can get from the Buckle of the Bible Belt, she was never taught that to have a relationship with God or to get to heaven, you have to go through Jesus Christ. This man from Tennessee *was* taught that and still believes it to this day. Joanne told me she'd asked him, "Have you ever looked outside your faith?" When he said no, she said, "Well, you've been indoctrinated." Wonder of wonders, that really hit home to him. Not that he'll do anything about it, but at least it made him realize that his religious beliefs were put *into* him, not sought and found *by* him.

So yesterday morning when I was online, reminding people about our next study group meeting, I stumbled upon Susan's message thread. That's when I decided to speak my truth about it as kindly, yet directly, as I could. I'm such a non-confrontational person, I tend to back off from conversations such as these, but she left the door wide open, so I walked though it. Hopefully, I did so with grace and love:

Hi again Susan,

I just re-read this message from you and thought it might be helpful for me to let you know that we respectfully do not agree that the only way to God is through Jesus. We do agree, as the Bible says, that God is Omnipresent, meaning in all things present everywhere, both seen and unseen. Therefore, we are not separate from God. We are each tiny parts of the awesomeness of It, like a drop of water is of the ocean.

The 15-word "New Gospel" from *Conversations with God* is this:

WE ARE ALL ONE. OURS IS NOT A BETTER WAY. OURS IS MERELY ANOTHER WAY.

I sincerely hope this doesn't offend you. I just wanted to set the record straight. I am not trying to change your mind and hope you find great solace in your faith, as do I in mine.

I don't think, however, that we are a good fit for you if you're looking only for teachers who continue to teach you what you already believe.

Blessings,

Annie

You've no idea how hard it is for me to say things like that to people. Upon waking this morning it kind of hit me that if this book gets published, my dad, who I love with all my heart, might actually read it. God only knows how worried he'll be about me if he does. The last thing I would want to do is cloud his last years on Earth, worrying about my soul. He already worries about me enough without adding *this* weight to his mind and heart. But my dad, too, was indoctrinated. I know he freely continues to choose to accept Jesus Christ as his Lord and Savior, but I don't think he ever looked outside the Christian faith at other options.

Regardless, his beliefs have served him well, and he has led a happy life—successful, perhaps, beyond his wildest dreams. And he has shared extremely generously of his success, making my sisters' and my life so much easier than any one of us probably deserved. He also shared his accounting skills generously with his clients when he owned his CPA firm.

I remember filing for him as a kid, and each tax return would have Dad's fee written in the upper corner in red pencil. The prices were different, and what I realize now that I didn't realize then is, he charged people in accordance with their income. The people who didn't have much money only got charged $5. Others who were a bit better off, maybe $8 or $10, and so on.

So my beloved father, who seems to believe the Five Fallacies About God, interestingly, in following Jesus Christ's teachings, has lived his life largely in denial of the Five Fallacies About Life—with kindness and generosity toward people from all walks of life. To me, that is the mark of a good man.

THE VOICE

Greg (Mumbai, India)

See all; judge nothing.
Hear everything; bless the noise.
Love everywhere; choose from the contrast.

You are constantly being surrounded by the means to walk on the path to your complete life. All you have to do is be aware of all of it, bless all of it, and love all of it. The way will be so apparent to you that choices will be as clear as a summer's day, decisions will be easy, and your course of action will be obvious.

Chapter 6, Lesson #4

Well, my friend, you may give yourself a great big pat on the back and a virtual hug from me because you've made it all the way to the last lesson in our book! I'm so grateful you chose to explore these ideas, and I hope you've gained a clearer, more fulfilling experience of this thing called life. At least I know we've given you plenty of food for thought!

Our final concept is, I think, a fitting one in that it leaves us with the invitation to keep an open mind for the remainder of our days here on Earth:

Your experience of yourself and your world would change overnight if you adopted, collectively, these FIVE STEPS TO PEACE:

1. ALLOW YOURSELVES TO ACKNOWLEDGE THAT SOME OF YOUR OLD BELIEFS ABOUT GOD AND ABOUT LIFE ARE NO LONGER WORKING.

2. EXPLORE THE POSSIBILITY THAT THERE IS SOMETHING YOU DO NOT UNDERSTAND ABOUT GOD AND ABOUT LIFE, THE UNDERSTANDING OF WHICH COULD CHANGE EVERYTHING.

3. ANNOUNCE THAT YOU ARE WILLING FOR NEW UNDERSTANDINGS OF GOD AND LIFE TO NOW BE BROUGHT FORTH, UNDERSTANDINGS THAT COULD PRODUCE A NEW WAY OF LIFE ON THIS PLANET.

4. COURAGEOUSLY EXAMINE THESE NEW UNDERSTANDINGS, AND IF THEY ALIGN WITH YOUR PERSONAL INNER TRUTH AND KNOWING, ENLARGE YOUR BELIEF SYSTEM TO INCLUDE THEM.

5. EXPRESS YOUR LIVES AS A DEMONSTRATION OF YOUR HIGHEST BELIEFS, RATHER THAN A DENIAL OF THEM.

Why, you may ask, are these statements about beliefs and understandings called "The Five Steps to Peace"? The answer is quite simple: All wars that have ever been fought on this planet have come about because of misunderstandings that were allowed to fester and take hold. And most, if not all, of those misunderstandings have been about how God and life really are. If we go back to Chapter 1, "The Basics," we see that a misunderstanding of the Three Statements of Ultimate Truth are at cause in most human conflict:

1. We are all One.

2. There's enough.

3. There's nothing you have to do.

And so we have come full circle in this series of lessons, as did much of Neale's conversations in the CWG Cosmology itself! Discussions of great spiritual truths tend to be like that—circular—because the most important points tend to come up again and again. And the single most important message of *Conversations with God* is the very first one we discussed:

WE ARE ALL ONE.

Please write in your journal or post on the website your answers to the following Self-Reflection Questions:

1. Do you think it would be possible for two parties to wage war if they both deeply believed and demonstrated that there is only One Life, and we are connected to It and through It?

2. Do you think it would be possible for two parties to wage war if they both fully understood and demonstrated that there's enough land, resources, and anything else they desire, for all to share?

3. Do you think it would be possible for two parties to wage war if neither put any requirements or conditions on the other? If each simply allowed the other to walk their own path?

The following are Action Steps for you to take over the next week and beyond:

1. Examine your beliefs about God and life to see if you have any that are no longer working.

2. See if there is something you don't understand about God and life.

3. Be open for new understandings about God and life to come forth.

4. Examine these new understandings, and if they feel true to you, include them in your belief system.

5. In all things, allow your highest beliefs to express in your thoughts, words, and actions.

Postscript

"Love your enemies." Sounds simple, right? I would bet there are very few adults on the planet who haven't heard the advice "love your enemies" at least once or twice. If that is true, what if each and every person who has heard this simple advice were to begin living by it? Would the world look differently than it does now? Could we finally co-exist peacefully?

Apparently, we've got a long way to go. The 2016 presidential election thrust us Americans into what may have been the most contentious presidential election of my lifetime. And if you want to see the Law of Opposites at work, there's no time quite as juicy as a presidential election season!

What struck me most this time around was how nasty the rhetoric became as the candidates made enemies of each other, hell-bent on swaying the masses into agreeing that they were right, and everyone else was wrong.

Yet I have to wonder, what if someone could have sat down with each of them and asked this question: "Is it possible that there is something you don't know, the knowing of which could change everything?"

What if that question were asked of *every* candidate in *every* election? If nothing else, it would be a clear indicator of who is pliable and who is not. Recall to mind the third level of knowing from *Friendship with God*: "There appear to be those who do not know, but who *think that they know*. They are dangerous. Avoid them." It is when we think we know everything there is to know about something that we become self-righteous, and I can think of no larger impediment to peace.

Peace begins in the open hearts and minds of individuals. When I am clear that I don't know everything there is to know and am willing to allow more information in, I am at peace in my mind. When I choose to love unconditionally and without attachments, I am at peace in my heart.

My animal communicator friend Kate Solisti says our companion animals teach us that both ways of loving are important. Dogs teach us unconditional love—love that endures no matter what someone thinks, says, or does. Cats teach us unattached love—love that depends on nothing and no one outside of ourselves to "complete" us. I know of no better de-stressor than spending quality time with a dog or cat. They have a wonderful way of bringing us back to peace because, as *Conversations with God* says, they often act with more integrity and greater consistency than human beings do. What gifts they are to us!

One of my most inspiring friends, John Viscount, author of *Mind What Matters* and writer of the multi-award winning film, *Admissions*, is the co-founder of *PeaceNow.com*, a group that is gathering one billion signatures to create peace ministries and departments in every country on the planet. If we were to divert a fraction of the resources we currently spend on departments of defense to departments of peace, who knows what changes we might start to see around the world? I would think the Five Steps to Peace or some version thereof would serve beautifully as guiding principles in these ministries . . . along with a healthy dose of unconditional, unattached love!

THE VOICE

Annie (Los Angeles, California)

Stay in your place of love.

Radiate love.

Send love.

Surround others with your love.

They may not feel it at the level of mind, but they will feel it/know it at the soul level. This is what is meant by "love your enemies." In truth, there is no such thing as "enemies," as we are all part of the One Unified Whole, the One God Made Man in the Flesh. Yet so many have fallen down the rabbit hole, as it were, they've forgotten everything that Jesus the Christ taught them. He, of all people, was one of the few in his day and time who said to love your enemies. It was not part of the Jewish tradition which was full of rules and regulations, this definitely not being one of them.

Especially in your modern-day politics—alas, as in politics throughout the history of politics—there have been obvious and sometimes extreme divisions. This is on purpose, of course, so that you, the people, can choose between the contrast. Therefore, it is best/most peaceful for you to not get too caught up in their rhetoric. Know that all choices lie before you, and simply choose the one, the person, who makes you feel the best—who lights you up the most. Enjoy the process. It's fun! And it allows each of you to more clearly define who you are. That is why so many people enjoy the political season. It helps refine your wanting. Fear not the hate mongering. Love always triumphs over fear.

So we have come full circle. Read and repeat our opening words:

Stay in your place of love.

Radiate love.

Send love.

Surround others with your love.

That is all. We are finished. Good news and good admonishment for a peaceful life!

AFTERWORD

"I don't want to be a master."

I'll never forget Greg saying that to me one day. "You *don't*?!" I exclaimed. "No," he said, adding, "It would be too boring."

I think Greg had the idea that in order to achieve enlightenment, he would have to do away with many of the fun things he loves to do. Things that, on the surface, may not look like activities a highly evolved person would choose to participate in.

This is where I differed in opinion, and truth be told, I think he probably agrees with me now. As he and I have happily delved into the messages of *Conversations with God* and how we can use them to create a better life, we haven't really changed who we are and what we do all that much. Sure, we are more impeccable with our word now, and we intentionally come from love in our thoughts, words, and actions—most of the time, anyway. But other than that, we're still essentially the same people.

We still love to go to parties, he enjoys watching his favorite baseball team, we go camping and hiking, and he follows his bliss scoring films, while I follow mine performing with my band. On the surface, we seem like anybody else who is living life to the fullest.

And that's exactly the point. When we understand how life works on both the physical *and* the metaphysical levels, and we choose to create our experience of reality in alignment with our highest understandings, that's *how* we live life to the fullest.

Life doesn't have to look a certain way before we love what shows up, by the way. We just choose to love life, *however* it appears. *We* show up in *life,* choosing to be joyful, loving, accepting, blessing, and grateful—no matter what happens. This means I am friendly and attentive, even (and often) when whoever I am interacting with is a complete stranger, because when we brighten another's day, we brighten our own. It really is that simple. When we allow our daily activities—whatever they happen to be—to come from this intentionally loving place, isn't that what being a master is all about? Yes, we fall short sometimes, but thankfully, we remember to live up to what we know, a little more each day.

It really is no different than mastering an instrument. You start out not knowing a thing about it, but because you're intrigued by the idea, you give it a try and begin your studies. If you continue to enjoy playing the instrument, you keep practicing daily to get better at it. If you don't, you drop it. Yet you will always have a fundamental understanding of the instrument that you can use for the rest of your life.

If you *do* choose to master the instrument, it doesn't change who you essentially are. It just changes the way you play it.

That's all we're doing here. Changing the way we play the game of life by showing up in the highest and best way we know how. Who could ask more of us than this?

—Annie Sims

RECOMMENDED RESOURCES

Recommended Recordings (Referenced)

Chapter 1, Lesson #4: "It Ain't Over Yet" by Jan Garrett and JD Martin.

Chapter 1, Lesson #4: "80 Acres of Stars" by Annie Sims.

Chapter 2, Lesson #3: "Don't Worry, Be Happy" by Bobby McFerrin.

Chapter 2, Lesson #4: "Love Is Who I Am" by Annie Sims.

Chapter 3, Lesson #4: "Say Goodnight" by Beth Nielsen Chapman.

Chapter 4, Lesson #4: "The Heart of the Matter" by Don Henley.

Chapter 5, Lesson #4: "Change Everything" by Annie Sims.

Additional Recommended Recordings

Flying High CD by Stowe Dailey Shockey.

One Heart CD by JD Martin.

Go Within CD by Annie Sims.

CWG Invitation CD by Neale Donald Walsch and Barry Goldstein*

"Center of the Heart" single by Annie Sims.

*If you need help quieting your mind in order to hear *The Voice*, this link will take you to a page where you can purchase a recording that guides you through Neale's "How to Have Your Own Conversation with God" process: *www.CWGInvitation.com*

Recommended Video/Film (Referenced)

Chapter 1, Lesson #1: *My Stroke of Insight*, TED talk by Dr. Jill Bolte Taylor.

Chapter 1, Lesson #4: *80 Acres of Stars*, music video by Annie Sims.

Chapter 3, Lesson #1: *The SouLogic Process*, explanation and video by Neale Donald Walsch.

Chapter 4, Lesson #4: *I Believe This Belongs to You*, music video by Ester Nicholson with Greg Sims.

Chapter 5, Lesson #2: *Dying to Know: Ram Dass & Timothy Leary*, documentary, directed by Gay Dillingham.

Chapter 6, Lesson #1: *Life After Life*, documentary by Peter Shockey.

Chapter 6, Lesson #4: *Admissions*, short film by John Viscount.

Recommended Reading

Action Step books by Neale Donald Walsch:

Chapter 3, Lesson #2: *What God Wants*

Chapter 3, Lesson #4: *Home with God: In a Life That Never Ends*

Chapter 4, Lesson #3: *Happier Than God*

Chapter 6, Lesson #1: *When Everything Changes, Change Everything*

Chapter 6, Lesson #2: *Communion with God*

Chapter 6, Lesson #3: *The New Revelations*

Referenced books by Neale Donald Walsch:

Chapter 3, Lesson #3: *The Conversations with God Companion*

Chapter 4, Lesson #3: *Moments of Grace: When God Touches Our Lives Unexpectedly*

Chapter 5, Lesson #3: *God's Message to the World: You've Got Me All Wrong*

Chapter 6, Lesson #1: *The Only Thing That Matters*

Additional books in the Conversations with God Cosmology by Neale Donald Walsch:

Conversations with God: An Uncommon Dialogue, Books 1, 2, 3, & 4

Friendship with God

Tomorrow's God

What God Said

Additional books in the Conversations with Humanity Series by Neale Donald Walsch:

The Storm Before the Calm

Action Step books by other authors:

Chapter 5, Lesson #4: *Illusions: The Adventures of a Reluctant Messiah* by Richard Bach.

Chapter 6, Lesson #1: *Eight Weeks to Optimum Health* by Dr. Andrew Weil.

Referenced books by other authors:

Chapter 1, Lesson #1: *My Stroke of Insight: A Brain Scientist's Personal Journey* by Dr. Jill Bolte Taylor.

Chapter 1, Lesson #2: *The Holographic Universe* by Michael Talbot.

Chapter 1, Lesson #3: *Loving What Is* by Byron Katie.

Chapter 1, Lesson #4: *The Source Field Investigations* by David Wilcock.

Chapter 2, Lesson #1: *The Law of Attraction: The Basics of the Teachings of Abraham* by Esther and Jerry Hicks.

Chapter 2, Lesson #2: *Flying High* by Calvin Lehew and Stowe Dailey Shockey.

Chapter 3, Lesson #4: *The Search for Bridey Murphy* by Morey Bernstein.

Chapter 3, Lesson #4: *Conversations with Cat; Conversations with Dog; Conversations with Horse* by Kate Solisti.

Chapter 5, Lesson #1: *Pain Erasure* by Bonnie Prudden.

Chapter 5, Lesson #4: *Autobiography of a Yogi* by Paramahansa Yogananda.

Chapter 6, Lesson #1: *Life After Life* by Dr. Raymond A. Moody, Jr.

Chapter 6, Lesson #4: *Mind What Matters* by John Viscount.

Other Works Cited (All works used by permission)

"Gregory Fisher's Treat Yourself to Your Best!" by Gregory Fisher, ©2016, CentaurSpirit Communications. *www.gregoryfisher.life.*

Flying High by Calvin Lehew and Stowe Dailey Shockey, ©2011, Outside the BLOX Media in association with Balboa Press and Scribe Book Company.

Autobiography of a Yogi, ©1946 by Paramahansa Yogananda, © renewed 1974, 1998 by Self-Realization Fellowship, Los Angeles.

Loving What Is, ©2002 by Byron Katie. Harmony Books, imprint of Crown Publishing, subsidiary of Penguin Random House.

PRAISE FOR WISDOM THAT WORKS:
THE CWG ONLINE SCHOOL

https://www.cwg.foundation/p/WtW

"Annie, thank you so much for your guidance, support, and encouragement throughout the course. It has deepened my understanding about God/Life by practicing each lesson in everyday life and re-reading the CWG Cosmology. It has been a rich and beneficial experience for me as I have been feeling joy, love, and excitement to create my life (and I will continue to do so). THANK YOU!"
—Akiko, Australia

"Your classes worked really well for me. They provided an efficient way to put the concepts of the CWG Cosmology in practice and weren't too time consuming for me (which is a factor to weigh in when you have two jobs, two kids, and an appetite for traveling!). Besides, you have a very refreshing, down-to-Earth way of explaining things. The examples you gave often stuck with me and helped a lot. Let me know if you're thinking about giving more of them because I'd be the first to enroll!"
—Sophie, France

"I say with more gratitude than words can express, Thank YOU!! I have been, hopefully, giving you the opportunity to be the great Bringer Of Light I see in you. You have succeeded wonderfully. I can never forget your dedication and true heartfulness to me and to us all."

—Michael, United States

"Thank you, Annie. I can't tell you in words how much I appreciate doing this course. The joy and wisdom that I obtain through it amazes me. I have found new vigor in studying the CWG material."

—Gerhard, South Africa

"Dear Annie, thank you for accompanying me on this six-month journey. I appreciate how you lovingly validated and supported me along the way. I have printed out all the lessons, as well as the questions and answers, and will return to them again and again to serve as a reminder."

—Erika, Canada

"I can't believe this is the last lesson! THANK YOU, Annie. This has been a profound and incredible experience, and these are the best homework assignments I've ever done!"

—Sangita, India

"I have loved this program deeply. I am so grateful for Neale, his work, and your work here, Annie. I will be a student of CWG for all the days of my life, and I know that I will assist others again and again to find their God within by sharing this."

—Alisse, Australia

ACKNOWLEDGEMENTS

There are far too many people to thank for helping me arrive at a place in my life that I could tackle the daunting task of writing a book and seeing it through to fruition. I fear that if I try to name everyone who has influenced me over the years, I'll accidentally omit someone. Therefore, I shall limit this book's list of acknowledgements to the people who directly supported me in creating it. Deepest gratitude to . . .

 . . . firstly, my online students, life coaching clients, and friends who generously shared their Postscript stories and *Voice* quotes. They are, in the order in which their writings appear in this book: Kim, Sophie, Cynthia, Allan, Laura, Greg, Donna, Akiko, Audrey, Ross, Gregory, Colleen, PJ, Neale, Kelly, and Marie.

. . . secondly, the friends who helped with editing and publishing advice. They are, in the order they showed up big to help: Greg, Darrel, Neale, Pamela, Aura, Peter, John, Laurie, Emily, Kate, and Sylvia.

. . . thirdly, the authors, musicians, videographers, and spiritual leaders whose works impacted my life in such an important way as to be included here. They are listed in this book's Recommended Resources section.

. . . lastly, you, the readers, for taking this extraordinary journey with me. I thank you from the bottom of my heart.

ABOUT THE AUTHOR

Annie Sims is a lifelong professional musician who has written and performed inspirational songs since 2005 when she and her husband, composer Greg Sims, traveled to eight countries in Europe with best-selling author of *Conversations with God*, Neale Donald Walsch, providing music for his lecture and workshop tour. Annie and Greg have won two awards in the New Thought Music genre: a Posi Award from emPower Music & Arts for their song, "Center of the Heart" (co-written with Jan Garrett), and a Seal of Excellence from the Positive Music Association for their CD, *Go Within*. Their song, "Change Everything," was included in a limited edition, signed, and numbered series of Walsch's book, *When Everything Changes, Change Everything*. Annie's music is available on iTunes and CD Baby.

Annie serves as secretary/treasurer of the Board of Trustees of the Conversations with God Foundation, as author/instructor of Wisdom that Works: The CWG Online School, and as co-facilitator of a bi-monthly Conversations with God Spiritual Study Group in Los Angeles. She is available for private consultations as a Conversations with God Life Coach and CWG tutor. To schedule an appointment please email: *annie@cwg.org*

For more information, please visit: *www.AnnieSims.com*

Rainbow Ridge Books publishes spiritual, metaphysical, and self-help titles, and is distributed by Square One Publishers in Garden City Park, New York.

To contact authors and editors, peruse our titles, and see submission guidelines, please visit our website at www.rainbowridgebooks.com.

For orders and catalogs, please call toll-free: (877) 900-BOOK.